Rural Development in China

Rural Development in China:

The Rise of Innovative Institutions and Markets

Volume 3

Lu Yilong

Enrich Professional Publishing

Honolulu • Hong Kong • Beijing • Singapore

Published by

Enrich Professional Publishing, Inc.
Suite 208
Davies Pacific Center
841 Bishop Street
Honolulu, HI, 96813
Website: www.enrichprofessional.com
A Member of Enrich Culture Group Limited

Hong Kong Head Office:
11/F, Benson Tower, 74 Hung To Road, Kwun Tong, Kowloon, Hong Kong, China

China Office:
Rm 309, Building A, Central Valley, 16 Haidian Middle Street, Haidian District, Beijing, China

Singapore Office:
16L, Enterprise Road, Singapore 627660

By Lu Yilong

With the title *Rural Development in China: The Rise of Innovative Institutions and Markets Volume 3*
Translated by Yu Lun
Edited by Cao Yue and Yu Lun

ISBN (Hardback) 978-1-62320-086-2
ISBN (pdf) 978-1-62320-087-9

Enrich Professional Publishing is an independent globally-minded publisher focusing on the economic and financial developments that have revolutionized New China. We aim to serve the needs of advanced degree students, researchers, and business professionals who are looking for authoritative, accurate, and engaging information on China.

Contents

12

Chapter

Rural Development in China: 1949–2009

Rural development has entered a new phase since the founding of PRC in 1949. Rural China is the foundation of new China, and farmers the heroes for founding their nation. Then, how has the new regime benefited rural development and rural residents? Clearly, noticeable changes have been brought to both villages and farmers' lives for the better over the past 60-plus years; yet at the same time, they have also experienced great difficulties and will continue to encounter numerous challenges. A review of the history of rural development will be beneficial for policymakers to draw lessons from past experience, address squarely problems occurred, and make plans for better rural development.

The launch of the Reform and Opening Up policy in 1979 marked a watershed in China's rural development. Review and analysis in this chapter will follow such a division for the benefit of historical comparisons.

Rural Development between 1949 and 1979: Experience and Problems

China's Reform and Opening Up policy was not put into place until late 1978 when the Third Plenary Session of the 11th CPC Central Committee was held. So, for the 30 years prior to this reform, how had rural China developed and what problems had the country encountered?

Rural revolution and rural construction are prioritized by China in its plan of national development, for villages are places where severe problems exist. As was pointed out by Fei in his investigation on rural southern Jiangsu in the 1930s, "the essential problem in Chinese villages, putting it in the simplest terms, is that the income of the villagers has been reduced to such an extent that it is not sufficient even to meet the expenditure in securing the minimum requirements of livelihood. It is the hunger of the people that is the real issue in China."[1] The new regime of the PRC, then, had to first deal with the tough issue of giving a fresh look to rural life and rural development, and this has become a significant part of government policy ever since. During the 30-year period from 1949 to 1979, the Chinese government had carried out a series of polices in the hope of pulling the countryside out of poverty and economic underdevelopment. Those efforts included: the land reform, collectivization of agriculture, the setting up of people's communes, the establishment of state monopoly on grain trade, as well as other reforms and measures aiming for the construction of a new socialist countryside. Bearing in mind the goal of changing rural life for the better, those attempts have played an exemplary role in dealing with the relationship between the government and villages as well as peasants. The following sections will discuss the effects of these reforms and what lessons could be drawn.

Land reform

Land is a key factor among the Three Rural Issues, therefore, after the birth of PRC in the 1949, the priority of rural development was given to the reform of land. Developed on the basis of the 1947 *Outline Land Law of China*, the *Agrarian Reform Law of the People's Republic of China* (hereinafter referred to as the *Agrarian Reform Law*) was promulgated, which confirmed that the land reform should be implemented by regions and by stages in rural areas.

The reform of the land system was carried out in an attempt to reverse the situation where the land was controlled by the minority, and equalize land rights among peasants to boost the efficiency of agricultural production. In this way, landless and land-deficient peasants would be entitled to a piece of land to build their life upon, thus realizing the goal of "land to the tiller".

The *Agrarian Reform Law* was the legal base for the land reform in the 1950s. The content of the land reform boiled down to three aspects: land confiscation and expropriation; land redistribution; and the establishment of an executive organ of the reform.

Land confiscation and expropriation target the private land and common land owned by landlords, migrated peasants, and organizations in villages. As stipulated in Article 2, Chapter 2 "Land Confiscation and Land Expropriation" of the law, farmland, draft animals, farming tools, and surplus crops and houses owned by landlords shall be confiscated. In Article 3, it further provided that rural common land and land occupied by ancestral halls, temples, churches, schools and other organizations shall be expropriated.

Regarding the redistribution of the confiscated and expropriated land and other means of production, the *Agrarian Reform Law* said that they shall be fairly distributed to poor peasants with no or little land in the same town. According to Article 10, Chapter 3 "Land Redistribution" of the law, "all confiscated or expropriated land and other means of production except that to be nationalized as set forth herein shall be taken over by the township peasants association and then allocated in a unified, fair and reasonable way to the poor peasants with a lack of land or without land or other means of production and to the landlords as well allowing them to maintain their life by working on their own and improve themselves at work."[2] Article 11 stated that, collectively owned land shall be redistributed equitably among rural households based on their original farmland conditions at the township or administrative village level, according to family size combined with the quantity, quality and location of land; and in this process, peasant associations at the district or county level shall help making necessary adjustments between towns or administrative villages.

Peasant congresses and peasant associations were recognized by law as the executive organ for carrying out the reform of land. As stated in Article 29 of Chapter 5, "Enforcement Authorities and Measures," peasant meetings, peasant congresses and committees of selected peasant associations at the village, town, district, county, and provincial level, shall be designated as legal executive organs of the land reform.

The land reform dramatically changed the allocation pattern of farmland and other major means of production. The target of this revolution was landlords, whose political and socioeconomic statuses were degenerated to be equal to or even inferior to those of poor peasants. Then naturally, poor peasants, with little or no land, were the biggest beneficiary of this reform.

The land reform has also significantly altered the social fabric of rural China. The expropriation of the common land occupied by religious and other groups took away their economic basis in rural areas. By cutting off the connection between rural land and economy and those non-peasant organizations, the reform has crippled the impact of external forces on rural society, afforded villages better autonomy, and assisted the new regime to consolidate its control over rural areas.

One more thing to note, this land reform neither fundamentally revamped the system of rural land tenure nor established collective ownership. Yet the executive organs and methods established by the *Agrarian Reform Law* did contribute greatly by laying political and legal bases for the building of collective ownership of rural land. Since the *Agrarian Reform Law* has given the rights to distribute and dispose of rural land to peasant congresses and peasant associations, both of which were actually in the charge of the central government. What was also stated in the *Agrarian Reform Law* is that, the reassignment and allocation of land should be conducted within the scope of towns or town-level administrative villages. This rule, in a sense, reinforced a town's role as a collective, that is, the government could better control and dispose of rural land through the hands of towns. This explains why the agricultural collectivization movement later could bring rural land under the control of people's communes, which were transformed from towns, and on what historical and social bases the collective land ownership system has developed in rural China.

Then, what made the redistribution of rural land in the land reform possible, since nobody was willing to hand over their land for redistribution? To achieve the goal of land reform, the government continued relying on rural grassroots. Rural residents were stratified and divided into various classes, such as landlords, rich peasant, and poor peasants. According to peasants' class status, the method of "drawing on the plentiful to make up for the scarce, and drawing on the fat to make up for the lean" (*chouduo bushao, choufei bushou* 抽多補少，抽肥補瘦) was applied through class struggle. As early as the period between 1946 and 1949, the class-struggle approach was already adopted in the agrarian reform in the old liberated areas. For example in Shilidian Village, rural households were classified into four classes, among which poor peasants and middle peasants were to be united with, while landlords and rich peasants were to be fought against. These labels, based on family landholdings and overall economic position, were made for the purpose of reallocating land to poor and landless peasants in proportion to what they deserved.[3]

The successful establishment of the new rural land tenure arrangements in rural China was inseparable from the help of political movements. As the new system almost revolutionized the entire pre-existing patterns for allocating land and other benefits, it was impossible for any single decree or law to push forward such a dramatic change. Therefore, in a sense, it is effective to make use of political campaigns to push through the reform of land system, for these campaigns did help embed and popularize the new land system in the vast rural areas.

Land reform proceeded step by step as planned in all new liberated areas from 1950 to 1952. East China had completed 82.1% of land reform projects by the spring of 1951, and 100% by the autumn of 1952.[4] In central, south, and southwestern China, where the land reform was carried out through three phases, all villages apart from those in minority areas had completed the reform by the end of 1952. In the same year, China basically finished the reform, except for the Tibetan habitations in Xinjiang, Qinghai, and Gansu, northwestern.[5]

This reform of rural land system completely changed the institutional basis of rural society, marking a new phase in rural development. Specifically, the land reform at the dawn of New China impacted the rural society in the following four aspects:

- Land reform laid the foundation for the government to control rural land. In the initial stage, the land reform did not deny land owners' right to possess and use land; what it did change was the way land was distributed to labor, that is, the pattern of land allocation. That the reallocation of land proceeded successfully means that China's new regime had the power to use and dispose of rural land. This power constituted the basis for establishing collective ownership of rural land.
- Land reform facilitated the effective integration of labor and land, and hence, raising the economic efficiency of agricultural production. Through redistributing land among rural households, landless and land-deficient peasants received their due shares of land, and thus the government's

promise of "land to the tiller" was fulfilled on a larger scale. With peasants all holding a piece of land, the economic efficiency of both labor and land got raised. Moreover, since the land was in their own possession, poor peasants were much more enthusiastic about farming than ever before, which greatly contributed to the upgrade of agricultural productivity.

- This land reform successfully restructured the rural society. Land is a key factor in agricultural production. The reallocation of land fundamentally changed the social relation and structure of rural China. This rural land reform has reshuffled the rural social strata, and significantly uplifted the economic, political and social standing of numerous poor and lower-middle peasants. In this reform, "The old elite was stripped of its economic assets.... The crucial fact was that the old order had proved powerless, and peasants could now confidently support the new system. The old village institutions of clan, temple, and secret society had been displaced by the new...."[6]
- Land reform laid a solid basis for consolidating the position of agriculture as the foundation of the national economy and further promoting China's all-round construction. Stable countryside and thriving agriculture are what supported China to get through the ever-changing internal and external challenges and still enables the country to manage to proceed with various other undertakings.

From a historical perspective, land reform has also helped build up a new set of orders in rural China. A problematic land system was a major source of three-rural and even national difficulties in the first half of the 20th century. A private ownership of land led to the over concentration of land uses, which caused a terrible labor-land separation, severe social stratification, and then a series of other social problems. Therefore, it is rational for the new regime to prioritize rural land reform after the founding of the nation. However, the political–campaign style of operation made this reform become less of an institutional innovation and more of a political movement, posing hazards to later rural development.

A major contribution of this land reform is that it allocated land to poor and middle peasants, and motivated the peasants to enthusiastically engage in farming, thereby promoting the agricultural productivity. This can be seen from the rise in China's food production (see Table 12.1 and Fig. 12.1).

Table 12.1 Food production during the land reform

Year	Total sown area (thousand hectare)	Grain crops		
		Sown area (thousand hectare)	Yield (thousand ton)	Yield per hectare (kg/ha)
1949	124,286.1	109,958.7	113,180.0	1,029
1952	141,255.8	123,978.7	163,915.0	1,322

Source: Ministry of Agriculture of the People's Republic of China, *Agricultural Statistics of the People's Republic of China, 1949-2008,* 17.

Fig. 12.1 Agricultural production during the land reform

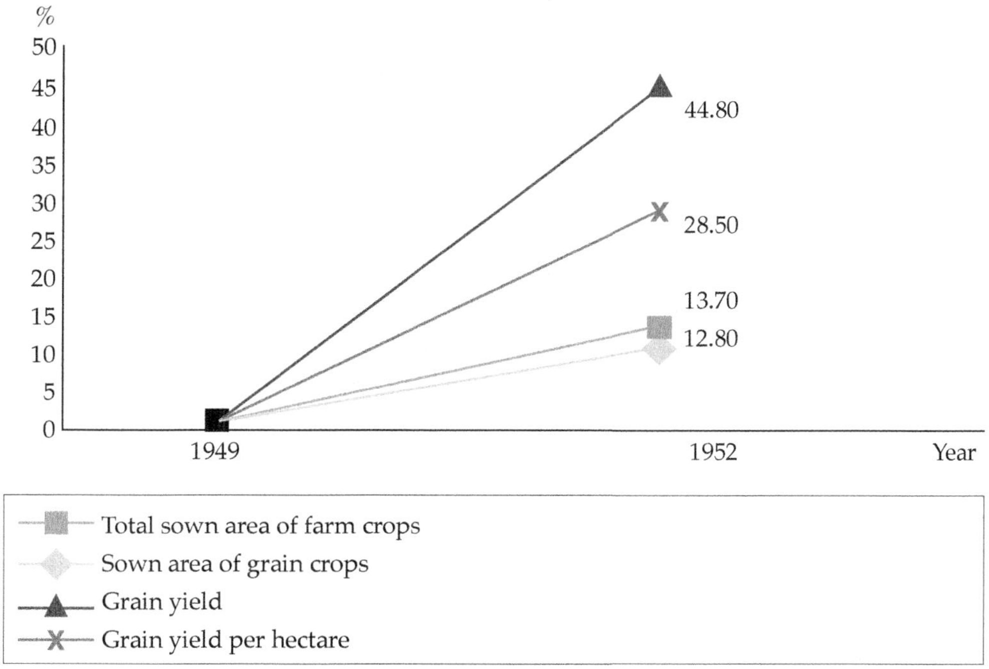

Source: Ministry of Agriculture of the People's Republic of China, *Agricultural Statistics of the People's Republic of China, 1949-2008.*

Figure 12.1 shows the changes of agricultural production from 1949 to 1952. The production of grain crops made the most progress: Total grain yield grew by 44.8% and grain yield per hectare increased by 28.5%. These figures indicate that, in the time of land reform, both the total output and productivity of farming grew significantly. Specifically, the increase in sown area was a major driving force for the rise in agricultural yield, and the land-reform–inspired farming initiative was accountable for the rise in per hectare yield.

The land reform in rural China did alter the nature and structure of land ownership, yet it did not change the system of agricultural production and management. After the reform, the government took control of farmland allocation, yet rural households could still independently decide and manage their production. This system of individual operation (*geti jingying* 個體經營), which granted rural households great autonomy in management and accounting, greatly helped restore agricultural production and the rural economy. That is why the rural individual economy (*geti jingji* 個體經濟) was still advocated in the *Ten Major Agricultural Policies* issued after the land reform. At that time, the strategy for agricultural development, as stated by the central Department of Agriculture and Industry, was to vigorously promote agricultural productivity on the basis of the current small-peasant economy.[7] This *Ten Major Agricultural Policies* allowed rural households to rearrange land, hire labor, take loans, and conduct free trade.

Farming operation with household being the basic unit, which is a form of small-peasant operation, is distinct from large-scale farming. This system of individual operation was adopted in a time when China had just started to recover from the wars and its agriculture had broken the shackles of the old system to embrace a new land system. Thus, it was not only justifiable but compatible with the laws of agricultural development to hold on to small-scale farming at that time when China's socialist agriculture was in its initial stage.

Agricultural production is different from industrial production. Industrial enterprises are able to effectively measure employees' job performance and then give rewards or penalties accordingly. A sound reward and punishment system can help the company establish an effective incentive mechanism, thereby raising employees' enthusiasm for work. In contrast, it is difficult to measure labor input in agricultural production. This is why large-scale collective farms often have trouble establishing an effective incentive system to stimulate peasants to put in more efforts. Individual rural households, on the other hand, have their own internal incentive systems, and therefore, an upper hand in boosting farming enthusiasm when compared to large-scale farms. Catering to the low agricultural productivity, this system of individual operation has significantly contributed to the recovery of agricultural production and the rural economy in the early years of the new China.

The system of individual operation fits China's situation as well. China has a huge number of villages that vary in terms of natural endowments, socioeconomic status, historical and cultural backgrounds, and conditions for future development. Then naturally, production and operation systems should differ and adapt to each place according to the local conditions. The individual operation system allows rural households to make rational decisions and rearrangements based on the reality, thus fulfilling the strategy of carrying out agricultural production in line with local conditions.

The essence of individual operation is to individual household as the basic production unit, which conforms to traditional farming production. From another perspective, as Zhou suggested, individual household is the natural unit of agricultural production.[8] This is because that firstly, the family bond makes household cooperation go on smoothly; secondly, it is more efficient to allocate farming duties within an household; and thirdly, the life cycle of a household matches the production cycle of traditional agriculture, making rural households a better answer to the needs of farming.

In times of China's socialist revolution, rural land reforms greatly contributed to the final success, and it helped the Communist Party of China (CPC) gain the support from peasants. And in the initial stage of China's socialist construction, it is still necessary to continue the reform of rural land system, whether or not such a reform could bring an optimal land system. That is because land remains the fundamental issue and the starting point of rural development. Given this, the reform of land system is the route China must take.

The land reform of 1949–1953 came to an overall good result in promoting rural and agricultural development. Conforming to the basic rules of rural development in the preliminary stage of socialism, the resulted land system cooperated well with the individual operation of rural households in raising the allocative efficiency of agricultural production factors, thus upgrading the level of productivity. Despite some political tints, which affected only a small minority of the population, this land reform was effective in boosting the peasant masses' enthusiasm for socialist construction.

Just like any other reform, this land reform is neither a cure-all nor a permanent solution. Social changes may render the once-fitted systems outdated and even destructive. With all the perks listed above, the land reform do have the shortcoming of defining land rights too general and ambiguous, thereby raising transaction fees in market exchanges to a great extent and exerting a negative impact on the increase of agricultural efficiency and peasants' income.

Rural land reforms in times of China's revolution and construction can be labeled as mandatory institutional changes, which lean on a new ideology for moral support and a new political power for practical support. Therefore, the land reforms exhibited a strong political nature. Under the social and historical backgrounds of that time, land reform acted as major "surgery" to the pressing issue of the society, that is, how the masses, especially poor and lower-middle peasants, could manage their livelihood. By reallocating rural farmland, the land reform has delivered the promise of "land to the tiller"; and with peasants' livelihood being secured, all sorts of social problems could be easily handled.

Land reform is not merely a change of land system in the sense of economics, but also a rural revolution. It has transformed the rural social order by solving the problem of uneven farmland allocation, thus taking on prominent political significance. However, it was not a priority at that time whether the rules of land possession and land use established through the land reform were effective in constantly promoting agricultural productivity. The utmost concerns were the well-being of rural households and the reconstruction of the social order — How can the poor and middle peasants make a living?; and how can the new regime and the new social order remain effective? Apparently, to address these issues, the government needs to first adjust the allocation of land resources, and let poor and lower-middle peasants have a fair share of farmland. The aim of this land reform was to mobilize the peasant masses to solve rural social problems, and in this process, restructure rural social order and consolidate the new regime.

From a historical perspective, this round of rural land reform mainly solved the imbalance of land allocation and the resulting social problems. So, the essence of this reform was to reassign farmland and other means of agricultural production in rural areas, or in other words, to remedy inequity in resource allocation. Yet, the government chose to "reshuffle" the distribution pattern of critical resources in a revolutionary manner rather than formulate strict rules of resource distribution in a forceful legislative manner. As a result, along with the reallocation of rural land, this reform disrupted the rules of land property rights and left the following issues unsettled: First, among the government, rural households and the later emerged rural collectives, who should hold the property rights of land?; second, how to deal with land property rights? The absence of answers led to the later-on troubles of policy uncertainty and deviation as well as an agricultural crisis.

Overall, the land reform in the early years of New China started a new phase of rural development, but in the meantime, its institutional ambiguity shadowed the future development of agriculture, rural areas and rural residents, and turned the development volatile and uncertain.

Agricultural collectivization

China launched its *1st Five-Year Plan* in 1953, stepping into the era of socialist economic construction and industrialization. To achieve the goals of the *1st Five-Year Plan*, the government must consolidate the role of agriculture as the foundation of the national economy and raise agricultural productivity to the next level. For policy makers, however, it seemed that the decentralized small-scale farming was what trapped agricultural productivity from further improvement. Accordingly, socialist transformation has been made the core mission of rural construction ever since the land reform. At first, the government tried cooperative farming between rural households to elevate production efficiency. By encouraging rural households to form mutual-aid teams, the government expected to elevate the level of cooperation between individual rural households.

Mutual-aid teams are made of willingly participated rural households, so this arrangement could have a positive impact on the improvement of household cooperation. Moreover, with the system of agricultural production and management as well as the rural interest pattern staying unchanged, mutual-aid teams will impact rural production relations and economic performance, mostly in a positive way. That said, the efforts of mutual-aid teams were still far from enough to push agricultural productivity and rural economic towards a qualitative leap. This was because that mutual-aid teams did not form stable and systematic division of labor. In mutual-aid teams, households helped each other in their faming, which was effective in lightening their workload and raising the efficiency of work at a particular period. But there was no division of labor, as seen in modern production organizations, between rural households or individual laborers. Modern division of labor can significantly boost productivity through distributing and coordinating different types of work among specialized industries. Consequently, as mutual-aid teams fell short of what the police makers had expected, developing agricultural cooperatives was put onto the government's agenda.

In 1953, Mao gave two important talks on mutual aid and cooperation in agriculture. In his speech on October 15, he noted:

> The rural work departments at all levels should look upon mutual aid and co-operation as a matter of vital importance. Peasants working on their own cannot raise production to any great extent, therefore we must promote mutual aid and co-operation. If socialism does not occupy the rural positions, capitalism inevitably will.[9]

On November 14, he further explained the significance of establishing rural cooperatives:

> Some people speak of the scattered nature as well as the hardships of the villages, that is, the scattered nature of the small peasant economy; but in doing so, they fail to mention forming co-operatives. To carry out the socialist transformation of the individual economy, to promote mutual aid and co-operation and to set up co-operatives — this is not merely the direction to take but the immediate task before us.[10]

In response to the call, the government started to promote the agricultural cooperative system in rural areas by encouraging villages to set up collectives and motivating peasants to join in. At first, primary cooperatives were experimented with. Rural households joined on a voluntary basis and took with them their land and large farming tools for the purpose of collective operation. For all member households, income was distributed according to their respective share of resource and capital inputs, as well as the amount of labor they pitched in. Primary cooperatives encountered many difficulties in their operation and management, especially in deciding the method of distributing income in relation to the inputs of capital, means of production, and labor. In primary cooperatives, farmland was pooled as shares for profit sharing, farming tools were used together among the members, rural households had the freedom to join and withdraw from the cooperatives;[11] yet unlike joint-stock companies, it was hard for primary cooperatives to accurately quantify shares and labor input. This difficulty in management led to the situation where very few rural households would voluntarily join primary cooperatives. It was especially true in areas where fellow households were not complementary in work. There, primary cooperatives could not display the advantages of cooperation and higher efficiency. Worse still, they would even spark off internal disputes over income distribution. How much should member-households get for their farmland input? How much for labor work? Is there a reward for offering farming tools? These were the problems which primary cooperatives found hard to settle. Worse still, if those problems were handled poorly, fellow members would hold a grudge against each other, or even deliberately stir up trouble, making cooperation even impossible.

Soon afterwards, China raised the level of agricultural collectivization by promoting advanced cooperatives in villages. Rural households no longer had the right to join and quit cooperatives at will. With the goal of bringing all rural households into cooperative agricultural operation, the government adopted a top-down political campaign to promote agricultural collectivization across the nation. As a political campaign, this movement forced all rural households to join cooperatives through political approaches and ideological propaganda. Take, for example, in Fengyang County of Anhui Province, villagers who refused to join advanced cooperatives would be vilified as timid and unenlightened "women with bound feet" (*xiaojiao nüren* 小腳女人), "capitalist roaders" (*zou zi pai* 走資派), and "drags on socialist construction" (*tuo shehuizhuyi houtui* 拖社會主義後腿). So, when some households were reluctant to bring their farmland and means of production into cooperatives, they would even chose to destroy their means of production such as killing their farming cattle.[12]

In advanced cooperatives, calculating the amount of labor work and distributing income became a big problem. Cooperative members often fought over the way work points shall be calculated, and furthermore, the method of income distribution stirred up even worse arguments. Some villages took compromised approaches, such as, for each individual rural household, cooperatives' income was distributed on the basis of 60% by work points and 40% by the number of laborers in the household. This approach was premised on the fact that farmland is equally distributed according to population. Labor work seemed to weigh heavier, yet in fact, income was still distributed according to the size of household population. Developing on the basis of small-scale farming, these agricultural cooperatives were combinations of rural households, not means of production. Therefore, the distribution of cooperative income could never be satisfactorily settled, and this led to an end result opposite to the expectation: Instead of smooth cooperation, rural households had to pay a higher management cost to work as a team.

Theoretically, advancing the division of labor can significantly boost efficiency. Yet, a beneficial cooperation works on two premises: Members have the complete autonomy to join and quit cooperatives by their free will; the management of cooperative organizations must be efficient. China's agricultural collectivization has neither of these two features, and thus, cooperatives failed in promoting cooperation, instead, it hurt the efficiency of human capital and working enthusiasm of individual rural households. The government forced collectivization into implementation by its political power; and this act, in fact, has only suppressed uncooperativeness, leaving behind potential hazards to collectivization. While agricultural collectivization has successfully pulled every rural household into agricultural cooperatives, it also put agricultural production into a latent crisis.

Agricultural collectivization was launched in the early years of new China, when agricultural productivity had progressed steadily and agriculture was just made the base of the national economy. This campaign was launched in an effort to advance the socialist transformation of ownership from the respect of production relations. The decision-making level of administration believed that small-peasant farming had become a constraint of yield increase, and to further boost agricultural productivity, it was necessary to replace scattered individual agricultural operation with large-scale agricultural production and cooperative farming.[13] In reality, however, it was quite difficult to change the scattered individual agricultural operation if the external environment had not been fundamentally changed; and rushing this process would bring more harm than good, despite the limited levels of cooperation and productive efficiency of small-scale farming. Then there came the dilemma of reforming traditional agriculture and promoting rural development: On the one hand, small-peasant farming was not efficient enough; yet on the other hand, it was not feasible to completely replace small-peasant operation with a more efficient mode of operation.

Another tip agricultural collectivization gives us is that: Political approaches would harm instead of boosting economic efficiency once they are used excessively, and worse still, the public's autonomy and enthusiasm would be discouraged by these political doings. People will find ways to promote efficiency, as long as they are given the liberty and right to make decisions. If cooperation proves to their advantage, people will voluntarily work together, and any administrative instructions and compulsory policies will turn out to be redundant and pointless.

The Great Leap Forward in agriculture: An illusion of rural reform

Through 1958 to 1960, China — from decision makers to the grass roots — was highly enthusiastic and optimist in the socialist construction. Specifically, people generally believed that the base of agricultural production was solid enough for making the leap into public ownership. As a result, the entire rural China started the Great Leap Forward movement by transforming advanced cooperatives into people's communes in an attempt to march to communism in one step.

The Great Leap Forward started from agriculture.[14] The Third Plenum of the Party's Eighth Central Committee approved the "National Programme of Agricultural Development from 1956 to 1967" (also called the Forty-Article Programme of Agricultural Development), which focused on the goals and methods of consolidating collective agricultural production and boosting yield increase. *People's Daily* then ran an editorial on this document, saying that all issues regarding agriculture and villages should head towards "a great leap forward." This editorial rang the bell of the Great Leap Forward in agriculture.

In response to the government's call for a complete overhaul of farmland irrigation and water conservancy infrastructure and the collection of manure for fertilizer, in January 1958, over 100 million people took part in rural construction, pushing the movement to a climax. The highly motivated enthusiasm of the massive rural population also effected the central policymakers, and as a result, this movement turned into a campaign of passion. Under such a background, in order to make the *2nd Five-Year Plan*, the Central Committee for Economic Affairs suggested the idea of setting two targets (*liangben zhang* 兩本賬) to Mao Zedong: one for the central government, and the other for local governments. The two targets can be further divided into a mandatory one which would be open to the public, and an aspirational one which would be kept confidential. This two-target planning strategy reflected a lack of transparency and honesty in the process of implementing a Great Leap Forward in agriculture across the country. With the presence of the two-target strategy, the central decision makers were able to put forward impracticably high demands, and local governments could also come up with ways to fabricate unrealistically satisfactory performance reports.

The central government called on local governments and all populace to try all means to raise agricultural yield and fulfill ahead of time the National Programme of Agricultural Development. In response to this call, all parts of the country began talking big about their agricultural production. Reports about unrealistic astonishing breakthroughs in rice, wheat, and corn production made by each region were frequently seen in *People's Daily*. It was obvious that these "breakthroughs" in output were nothing more than lies. The reason behind these vastly exaggerated figures was the two-target strategy: Local governments had to fake an agricultural yield to meet the impractical target set by the central government, and in the meantime, keep a record of the target they had actually met. The seemingly unbelievable fact that transparent lies were repeatedly posted in authoritative newspapers was a reflection of how the Great Leap Forward had twisted economic plans into political assignments and how the passion for political campaigns had driven the society to lose its sense of rationality. In such an irrational society, it was hard to ensure the smooth operation of the economy. However, in many villages where local residents believed that they had realized communism, members of people's communes were allowed to "eat from the same communal pot" (*chi daguofan* 吃大鍋飯) without paying anything. All these made people regard agricultural production as less important, sowing the seeds of the later three-year agricultural crisis.

It is perplexing why this blundering act of the Great Leap Forward could sweep the nation. Was it a result of political policies, or was there a broad public basis supporting these policies? According to some western scholars, the answer was the Chinese Communist movement.

> The motivations producing the Great Leap Forward strategy drew from very deep currents in the history of the Chinese Communist movement....

> A developmental dilemma, combined with dissatisfaction over the social consequence of the Soviet model, produced the search for a mobilizational alternative to previous practice. Organizational tensions between the Party and state apparatuses and between basic level governmental and economic units in the countryside added to the stresses.[15]

The upper echelons were the major driving force behind the Great Leap forward. These decision-makers intended to make use of people's enthusiasm and motivated them to devote themselves into the economic construction — just like the way they devoted to the socialist revolution, so that China could shake off its slow economic growth, and catch up with and even surpass Western countries within the shortest time possible. What is also worth noting is that the broad support from the masses in policy implementation shows that the government has successfully mobilized the masses and built a solid social basis for its actions. By using the mobilizational strategy combined with the coercive power from the central government's policies, the new political elite of grassroots rural society extensively promoted the practices of the Great Leap Forward in the vast rural areas. The grassroots, especially the grassroots elites, were just like the link connecting between the central government and the basic level of society, and have been so ever since the land reform. These grassroots cadres or political elites would help promote central policies in the local villages and at the same time, report local conditions and peasants' appeals to the upper levels of administration. Therefore, the messages they passed on to their superiors actually represented the demands and suggestions of the local people. Yet in the process of delivering messages between the upper cadres and the grassroots, the grassroots cadres or political elites always acted in the interests of the upper echelons, making them a pushing hand behind the poor decision-making and irrational measures in the periods of the agricultural collectivization and the Great Leap Forward.

Rural grassroots cadres were under political pressure to follow the government's principles and policies. But when unfeasible policies were blindly followed and even lavishly praised rather than firmly opposed, collective irrationality would inevitably be triggered.The Great Leap Forward is doomed to fail from the very beginning, because the decision-makers clearly knew that some of the targets in their plans were impossible to meet, yet these targets were released anyway for the purpose of increasing public motivation. When grassroots authorities started racing to talk big, the entire nation got trapped into a vicious cycle where nobody are willing to speak out the open secret. What followed the Great Leap Forward was the three-year agricultural crisis, which caused a devastating famine and eventually woke the nation from the fanaticism of the Great Leap Forward.

Although the subsequent Three Years of Great Chinese Famine was largely a result of a series of natural disasters, human mistakes and nationwide blind enthusiasm that accompanied the Great Leap Forward were believed to be key factors inducing the famine and the resulting social consequences. The pretentious and deceptive social environment made it impossible to size up the actual situation of agricultural production and grain supply, and it was no wonder that agriculture production decreased and the society had no capability to cope with the natural disasters.

People's communes

In 1958, China started the people's commune campaign with the feverish enthusiasm raised during the Great Leap Forward, under the propaganda of "People's commune is good" (*renmin gongshe hao* 人民公社好). People's communes are rural organizations that serve both political and economic purposes. Villages raced to announce the direct transformation into people's communes from advanced cooperatives or even primary cooperatives; and soon afterwards, the system of people's communes was established throughout the country. By the end of 1958, over 740,000 advanced cooperatives disappeared, over 99% of rural households enrolled in more than 260,000 people's communes.[16] Since then, rural China has stepped into the phase of people's communes.

Peasants accepted the brand new people's commune system with great enthusiasm and expectation, for they were told by the propaganda campaigns that people's communes would afford them a bright future. For one thing, the Communist Party stated clearly in the "Resolution on the Establishment of People's Communes in the Rural Areas" that "the people's Commune are the best form of organization for the attainment of socialism and gradual transition to communism. They will develop into the basic social units in the [future] communist society."[17] For another, local and grass-roots governments depicted a bright blueprint for their people upon the establishment of the people's commune system by promising a new socialist countryside where peasants could all live in apartment buildings instead of cottages, have telephones at home, light rooms with electric lamps, enjoy good living conditions, and live a harmonious and peaceful life.[18]

The people's commune system established the public ownership of the means of production, namely land and other means of agricultural production are collectively owned. In terms of economy, people's communes implemented "a three-level system of ownership with the production team as the foundation" (*sanji suoyou, dui wei jichu* 三級所有，隊為基礎). That is to say, means of production and products of labor were owned by three-level collectives: communes, production brigades, and production teams and the production team was taken as the basic accounting unit where collective production and distribution were performed. In terms of rural management, the people's commune was the grassroots administrative organ, managing public affairs in villages.

The implementation of the people's commune system also induced a switch of the system of agricultural production and management to a collective style. As a representative of farming collectives, the people's commune also is the owner of means of production, the basic-level unit of production, as well as the grassroots administrative organ. Theoretically, the people's commune system can pool individual rural households into large collective organizations and reach better labor productivity though labor division and cooperation. In reality, however, the collective distribution system still cannot balance the relationship between collective labor and individual labor. As a result, people's communes forced all laborers to stay in collectives at the expense of the individual members' creativity, since it was hard to decide which ones should or should not work outside.

From the above, it is clear that the people's commune system has damaged individual peasants' creativity and stifled future rural development, despite its success in removing certain barriers in cooperation. This is also the reason why the people's commune campaign has met its goal of ownership reform yet caused China a huge crisis instead of a boost in economic efficiency. Shortly after the people's commune system was implemented in rural China, a large-scale crisis attacked China's agricultural and rural development from 1959 to 1961, leaving agricultural production and food supply in a predicament.

Lessons learnt from the people's commune campaign suggests that it is utopian to expect the reform of economic ownership to be a cure-all for problems in the small-peasant economy. Neither agricultural cooperatives nor people's communes seemed to be effective in creating better cooperation between individual small peasants, despite the fact that the latter has successfully changed the system of ownership. Or maybe, it is unfeasible in the first place to attempt an efficient rural collective operation. After all, the village is not a modern enterprise but a big society made up by small peasants. In a modern enterprise, the target of its organizational system is individual economic men; in a village, however, the target is a social complex which consists of individual rural households. Therefore, it is sheer fantasy to change the face of rural China with a single reform of system.

To get rid of this agricultural crisis, the central government had to readjust its policies of collectives and collectivization. The adjustments were mainly in three aspects:

- Allow, to a certain extent, individual production and operation. For example, to restore "responsibility fields" (*zeren tian* 責任田) to rural households, and encourage them to operate independently on their own piece of land.

- Improve agricultural science and technology, and raise the role of technology in agricultural production. In 1963, the CPC Central Committee held a meeting on rural work, formally making improving agricultural science and technology an important strategic goal of agricultural development. This decision stands out as a notable landmark in the history of China's agricultural science, for the upgrading of agricultural science is of immense importance to the promotion of agricultural productivity and the adequacy of food supply for China's vast population. It is especially necessary for China's severely troubled agricultural industry to seek breakthroughs from scientific advancement.
- Channel more recourses into agriculture. In 1962, the national finance department allocated CNY3.82 billion to agriculture, accounting for 12.5% of the total fiscal expenditure, 5 percentage points higher than that in the 1st Five-Year Plan period; in 1965, national agricultural expenditure rose to CNY5.5 billion, 11.8% of the total fiscal expenditure.[19] In terms of rural infrastructure investment and newly increased fixed assets in farming, forestry, animal husbandry and fishery, during the period of the 1st Five-Year Plan, the former was CNY4.18 billion and the latter CNY3.45 billion; during the 2nd Five-Year Plan period, the two items rose to CNY13.57 billion and CNY8.64 billion respectively; and from 1963 to 1965, the two stood at CNY7.45 billion and CNY6.06 billion, respectively.[20] Thus it can be seen that China has significantly raised its investment in agriculture since the 2nd Five-Year Plan period.

With policy adjustment and the relentless efforts of the masses, agricultural production generally recovered from the crisis and the yield of grain production rose back to the level prior to the Great Leap Forward. In 1962, the national grain yield reached 308.8 billion catties [154.4 billion kilograms] and the average per capita yield was 480 catties [240 kilograms], quite close to the level in 1952; in 1965, these two figures rose to 389 billion catties [194.5 billion kilograms] and 544 catties [272 kilograms], respectively; and in 1978, 609.5 billion catties [304.75 billion kilograms] and 637 catties [315.8 catties]. Within just more than a decade, China's grain yield has successively broken the targets of 300 billion, 400 billion, 500 billion and even 600 billion catties.[21]

Grain yield is an important indicator of rural economic operation, and it can also reflect the effect of relevant rural policies. Fig. 12.2 demonstrates how China's grain production had developed prior to the implementation of the Reform and Opening Up policy. Apart from the period of the Great Leap Forward (1958–1961) when grain yield dropped significantly, the nation's grain yield was on the rise in all other years during this thirty-year period. This fact further proves that the campaigns of the Great Leap Forward and people's communes has produced marked negative effects, and the subsequent system of rural collective economy, in spite of its low efficiency, still managed to keep grain yield rising, just at a slower pace. It is probably owing to the steady growth in food production is what kept China's social orders rather stable even in times of the devastating political campaign of Cultural Revolution.

Fig. 12.2 China's grain production before the launch of the Reform and Opening Up policy

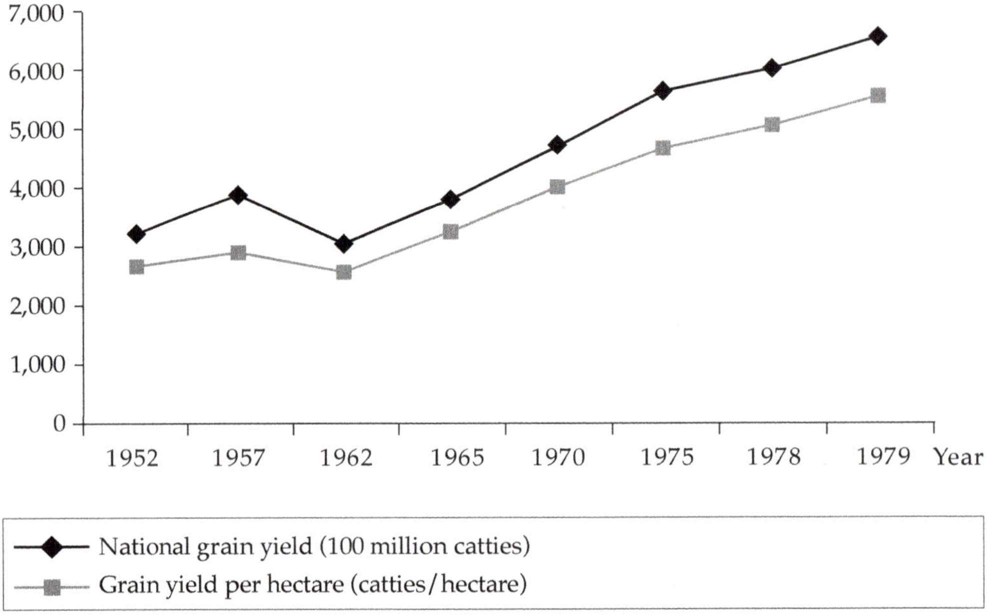

Source: Ministry of Agriculture of the People's Republic of China, *Agricultural Statistics of the People's Republic of China, 1949-2008.*

Rural Development in 1979–2009: Dilemmas and Solutions

In people's communes, peasants not only did not get wealthy, but had to struggle to feed themselves, and therefore, beating destitution was the prime goal and primary motivation for rural reforms.

Da baogan system

China's reform started with rural reform, and rural reform began from the *da baogan* 大包幹(contracting everything to households) reform. In 1978, 18 peasants from Xiaogang Village in Fengyang County, Anhui Province made a secret agreement to divide village-owned land into private family plots, which pioneered the reform of *da baogan*. According to their understanding, this meant that they each were responsible for their own plot, handing in part of the yield to the state and the collective, and keeping the rest for themselves. This reform in Xiaogang Village made immediate progress. Within the first year of implementation, *da baogan* had successfully pulled villagers of Xiaogang Village out of destitution. After that, the village ceased depending on the government for food, livelihood and agricultural production, and the efficiency of local agriculture production rose significantly.[22] The success of Xiaogang Village was gradually endorsed by the central government, and starting form 1979, the *da baogan* system was promoted across the nation. This movement, then, started waves of rural reforms in which the *da baogan* system (also known as the household responsibility system [*jiating lianchan chengbao zeren zhi* 家庭聯產承包責任制]) was at the core. With the deepening of rural reforms, people's commune system came to an end in 1984, giving way to a township system.

Da baogan or the household responsibility system, in essence, has restored the practice in which rural households have the right and autonomy to use and operate on farmland. In this way, rural households could make the full of their human capital and apply their talents and hard work to boost their production efficiency and labor income.

Rural reforms affected not only the economy, but also the relation between economy and politics. Along with the dissolution of the rural collective operation system, the political power embedded in the collective economy shrank dramatically. The ideology of class struggle has gradually handed the throne over to economic construction, and political approaches were substituted by rational choice making in economic development. The priority of rural society has switched from class struggle to economic construction, which were strong driving forces for reforming the rural social structure.

Since shaking off the political and economic constrains from collectives, rural laborers have restored and developed their autonomy and creativity. Starting from the mid-1980s, township enterprises have sprung up in the southeastern coastal areas, setting off an upsurge of industrialization in rural China. In Zhejiang and Jiangsu provinces, the rural industry grew with individuals contracting to operate commune- or brigade-run enterprises which were left over from the age of collective economy, and soon afterward, many more farmers followed suit and started their own businesses. The fast growing rural industry reshaped the economic structure in many rural areas by turning it from an agriculture-centered to industry- or non-agriculture–centered one. Clearly, rural reforms has sped up the process of rural industrialization. After the reforms, rural households were given bigger room to make full use of their human capital and household resources. Not only were they allowed to make own decisions about the model of agricultural operation, they also could choose to conduct non-agricultural businesses according to their own family conditions. Overall, the significance of the rural reforms lies in the effect of freeing rural laborers to fully bring out their work enthusiasm, initiative and creativity, which, to a large extent, helps promote the development of rural productivity and economy.

The immediate effect of *da baogan* in beating destitution shall be attributed to the restoration of the production and operation of individual rural households. The success of the reforms also proves that any attempt to change traditional agriculture would face grave risks, if it fails to preserve the independence of individual rural households. In other words, the independence of individual rural households is the premise of every rural reform.

It is because the *da baogan* system has found a balance in the relationships between farmers and the collective and between farmers and the state that this reform became a quick relief for peasants who were suffering from the trauma of agricultural collectivization and the people's commune system. In the time of the collective economy, the relationships among these parties were often ambiguous and complicated. Normally, ordinary members in a people's commune were unclear of how high the commune's agricultural yield was, how many responsibilities they should shoulder, and how much they could benefit from the commune. These unclear production relations could never motivate individual peasants' enthusiasm in farming work. The *da baoga*n system gave the responsibilities of farmland management and agricultural production back to rural households and cut off their reliance on the government and collective in farming. Under such a system, individual rural households needed to fully exert their capability and initiative to strive for better harvests and a higher living standard, for they had to take full responsibility for their life and production. This change was proved to be positive, as China's rural economy soon recovered once rural households had unlashed their farming potential and maximized grain yield.

The *da baogan* system was criticized as a retrogression in history upon its first release, but in fact, it was a return to reason. *Da baogan* has shattered the utopian idea that the people's commune system could bring in communism to rural China, and at the same time, it has proved that any impractical and rule-breaking attempts to transform small peasantry will be doomed to failure. Only with down-to-earth spirit and step-by-step work, can the efforts to promote rural development be positively effective. It is unrealistic to expect the modernization of agriculture, rural areas and farmers (collectively known as three rural issues) to happen overnight. Socioeconomic transitions will be a gradual process, so is the reform of small peasantry. In villages where modern agriculture has not been popularized, it complies with the laws of production to stick to individual households as the basic unit in farming, for in a loosely organized rural society, households are the effective units of economic activities.

Rural development after decollectivization

The system of household responsibility system gradually replaced the collective operation system with the deepening of rural reform. In 1984, the people's commune system came to a close, marking the end of the age of collective operation and announcing a change in grassroots rural management.

Thanks to the popularization of the household responsibility system, agricultural production has overcame low efficiency and rural households' farming enthusiasm has once again been restored and elevated. China's agricultural economy has been revived since the early 1980s. In particular, grain production has made impressive progress with both grain acreage and yield rising significantly. In 1978, the national grain yield reached 609.5 billion catties [304.75 billion kilograms], and in 1998, this figure grew to 1,024.6 billion catties [512.3 billion kilograms], with the per capita yield of 800 catties [400 kilograms].[23] This great improvement largely resolved the supply-demand imbalance in grain production as well as the subsistence problem.

With the quick growth in grain production, farmers soon walked out of destitution. Most of them could manage to feed the whole family by independent agricultural production and management, and absolute poverty was significantly relieved in rural areas. Before the implementation of the Reform and Opening Up policy, around 250 million people across China were stuck in absolute poverty and was struggling for food and clothing. By 1985, the Chinese population living under absolute poverty dropped to 125 million, only half that seven years ago, with an annual reduction of 17 million. In 2007, this figure further shrank to 14.79 million. Regarding the poverty headcount ratio, the ratio before the launch of the Reform and Opening Up policy was 30%, and plummeted to 14.8% and 1.6% in 1985 and 2007, respectively.[24]

The deepening of rural reforms accelerated the development of rural economy, thereby driving up the living standard of rural residents. Within just the first decade after the reform, farmers have stepped up from being sufficiently fed and clothed towards being fairly well-off. For example, from 1978 to 1991, farmers' per capita net income increased by 4.3 times from CNY133.6 to CNY708.6, with an average annual growth rate of 9.3% in real terms; per capita consumption expenditure rose from CNY116.06 to CNY619.79; the Engel coefficient dropped 10.1 percentage points from 67.7% to 57.6%.[25] As demonstrated by these statistics, rural households have seen a significant rise in their income, consumption and living standard over the course of a decade.

What is also worth noting is that township enterprises have sprung up since the mid-1980s. Booming township enterprises have changed the development landscape in many rural areas and strongly pushed forward the national economy. By 2003, China has over 21.85 million township enterprises with 135 million employees and CNY1.523 billion worth of total output, 8.49% more than the previous year.[26] Township enterprises have brought a qualitative leap in development to many villages and helped the residents lead a well-off life.

Township enterprises also significantly advanced the level of rural industrialization, which has fundamentally changed the social structure and the way of life in rural areas. In southern Jiangsu Province, for example, township enterprises created an outlet for the massive rural surplus labor, and by mid-1990s, roughly two thirds of rural labor have become their employees.[27] It is obvious that villages with prosperous industry were no longer earthbound, despite remaining being called "villages" according to the administrative division.

Starting from 1992, the rural reform has further deepened and widened to center around the construction of socialist market economy. This socialist reform opened up tremendous opportunities for rural development, and an increasingly open and prosperous rural market also gave farmers a better chance of development. Farmers gradually learned to adjust the structure of farming operation according to market demand, and many of them even started diversified operation by combining farming and sideline production, thus the reliance on yield and price rises to boost household income was diminished. Many rural families have successfully raised their income by either transferring their surplus labor (created by the division of labor within each household) to non-agricultural jobs, or conducting specialized, large-scale operation. As a result, in the second ten-year period after the introduction of the Reform and Opening Up policy, rural society has basically become well-off. From 1991 to 2000, per capita net income of rural households rose to CNY2,253 from CNY708; per capita consumption expenditure raised to CNY1,670 from CNY620; and the Engel coefficient dropped to 49.1% from 57.6%.[28]

In view of the trend of development, China's rural development will embrace a new era of great opportunities in the 21st century, and rural society and farmers will step into a new phase of development. The fact that rural development has made such impressive progress is not a mere coincidence but has a solid material basis. As long as the macroeconomic policies are in the right direction, goals of rural development will be met and a comprehensively well-off society will be built. First, grain production have been steadily increasing for several consecutive years and agricultural policies remains consistent, which materially guarantees all kinds of other rural undertakings. Second, the policy to promote urban-rural integration will afford the massive rural residents with better social benefits by sharing the fruits of the Reform and Opening Up policy. And finally, as macroeconomic regulation and control has shift its focus to stimulating domestic demand, villages and farmers will get more and better opportunities in the market.

Table 12.2 Changes in the consumption level of rural households by income quintile (CNY/person)

	Low-income household (20%)	Lower-middle-income household (20%)	Medium-income household (20%)	Upper-middle-income household (20%)	High-income household (20%)
1980	105	126	152	190	261
1990	332	440	538	668	1,018
2000	977	1,233	1,501	1,877	3,086
2005	1,548	1,913	2,328	2,879	4,593
2008	2,145	2,653	3,286	4,191	6,854
2008 over 1980 (times)	19.4	20.1	20.6	21.1	25.3
Average annual growth from 1980 to 2008 (%)	11.4	11.5	11.6	11.7	12.4

Source: Department of Social and Economic Survey, National Bureau of Statistics of China, *China Rural Statistical Yearbook 2008*, 315–27.

Table 12.2 reflects the changes in the quality of rural life during the 30 years after the implementation of the Reform and Opening Up policy. As shown in the table, rural households at different income levels have all led a much better life during the three decades of development, and the level of consumption has increased by almost 20 times.

The 21st century: Building a new socialist countryside

Upon entering the 21st century, the pressing issue of an underdeveloped countryside has become even more prominent. Specifically, urban-rural disparity is worsened, the improvement of farmers' income becomes even harder, and the uncertainty in the development of farmers is on the rise. To break the dilemma of rural development, the Chinese government has taken immediate measures in the following two respects. First, the state issued a series of positive fiscal and tax policies as well as administrative measures, which have effectively stopped the collection of unauthorized fees and relieved farmers from heavy burden. From 2001 to 2004, China has reduced and exempted agricultural tax by CNY23.4 billion, waived CNY6.8 billion of taxes on special agricultural products (excluding tobacco), and approved tax relief for natural disasters of CNY16 billion, among which CNY8.5 billion was fixed by the central government and CNY5 billion of social relief and CNY900 million of other relief including that for major grain growers were given by agricultural revenue collecting agencies at different levels. In 2005, the state further alleviated farmers' burden by offering a tax cut of CNY22 billion. By 2006, the start of the 11th Five-Year Plan period, agricultural tax had been completely abolished, relieving farmers from agricultural tax burden of around CNY220 per capita, CNY100 billion in total. The repeal of the over 2000-year-old agricultural tax marks a transition in the relationship between the state and farmers from demanding to giving. Since then, the agriculture-industry and urban-rural relationships have transformed into ones where industry nurtures agriculture and urban areas support rural areas, quite the opposite from the past. Second, the State has also channeled increasingly more investment into agriculture and villages with the aim of raising farmers' income. Constant improvement in rural infrastructure, such as transportation and communication, has created favorable conditions for the thriving of the rural economy and the better-off of farmers.

In 2006, constructing a new socialist countryside was made a major national strategy for both now and the near future. This strategy aims to realize the goals of "advanced production, improved livelihood, a civilized social atmosphere, clean and tidy villages and democratic administration." This proposal is made in accordance with the demand of the age and the characteristics of globalization, marketization, as well as rural development.

The fundamental policy of building a new socialist countryside is "giving more, taking less, or even taking nothing." "Giving more" means that the central government will fully support rural social and economic development. In terms of construction of infrastructure, the central-financed projects "to give every village access to highways as well as power and communications" have significantly improved the living conditions of rural residents and greatly developed the rural economy. In terms of agricultural production, the agricultural tax has been abolished and farmers are given subsidies for growing grains and other staple crops, which have allowed farmers to directly benefit from agricultural production and enormously aroused their enthusiasm in farming. Since 2006, the state has completely exempted tuition and miscellaneous fees for students receiving compulsory education in rural areas, significantly lightening the burden of rural households in education. In terms of social undertakings, the newly reformed system of rural cooperative medical care gives rural health care service a fresh look. In 2009, the state launched a reform in China's old-age insurance system to extend the coverage to all rural residents, and this reform will open up new horizons in the undertakings for the aged.

The Third Plenary Session of the 17th Central Committee of the CPC put once again rural construction and development in a crucial position by passing the *Decisions of the Central Committee of the Communist Party of China on Several Major Issues on Promoting the Reform and Development of Rural Areas* (hereinafter referred to as the *Decisions*). The *Decisions* urges vigorous efforts to strengthen the system building in rural areas and make breakthroughs in the key links of the structural reform of rural areas. Specifically, it is necessary to stabilize and improve the basic agricultural operation system, build a sound and standard rural land management system, intensify support and protection for agriculture, establish a modern rural finance system, improve the mechanism of integrated development of urban and rural areas, and perfect the rural public management system. What is also noteworthy is that the *Decisions* proposes to improve farmers' contracted land-use rights and protect their rights to occupy, use and get income from land contract; establish a unified public service system in urban and rural areas; and promote the balanced allocation of public resources between urban and rural areas.

The process of building a new socialist countryside shows that the government is playing an increasingly big role in rural affairs. Following the past style of rural reforms would inevitably put the new countryside construction into a structural dilemma. The right way is to promote rural development using the strategy of urbanization.

As shown in Fig. 12.3, the household responsibility system has effectively elevated agricultural efficiency ever since its implementation in the early 1980s. The first half of the 1980s saw grain yield soaring past 800 billion catties [400 kilograms], which has pulled the Chinese people out of the struggle for food and clothing. The other half of the 1980s, in contrast, witnessed a slight decrease in grain production. This reduction was attributable to two factors: First, the short-term effect of rural reforms has died away; and second, rural industrialization and urbanization have attracted much rural labor away from farming and the consistently low prices of grain products further dampened farmers' enthusiasm for crop planting. The rise of grain production and the agricultural economy since mid-1990s should be credited to the reform towards a socialist market economy, as well as the opening of secondary and tertiary grain markets. In 1998, the national grain yield still managed to hit 1 trillion catties [500 billion kilograms] in the face of the Asian financial crisis and the catastrophic floods in southern China. The subsequent resumption of the state monopoly on grain procurement, however, dramatically dragged down grain yield for it discouraged farmers from pursuing farming. This downturn of agricultural production has not been reversed until the re-opening of grain markets and the issuing of a series of preferential policies (for example, tax cuts). In 2007, which is the second year since the issuing of the strategy of building a new socialist countryside, the national grain yield again hit 1 trillion catties [500 billion kilograms] and this growth momentum continued for years. The above facts show that the steady growth of grain yield is a solid premise for maintaining the basic role of agriculture in the national economy. It is the sound growth of grain production that has helped the country through the 2008 global financial crisis, and paved the way for the "soft landing" of China's economy.

Looking back over the process of rural development since the launch of the Reform and Opening Up policy, the market-oriented reform has afforded farmers not only

Fig. 12.3 *China's grain production since the start of the Reform and Opening Up policy*

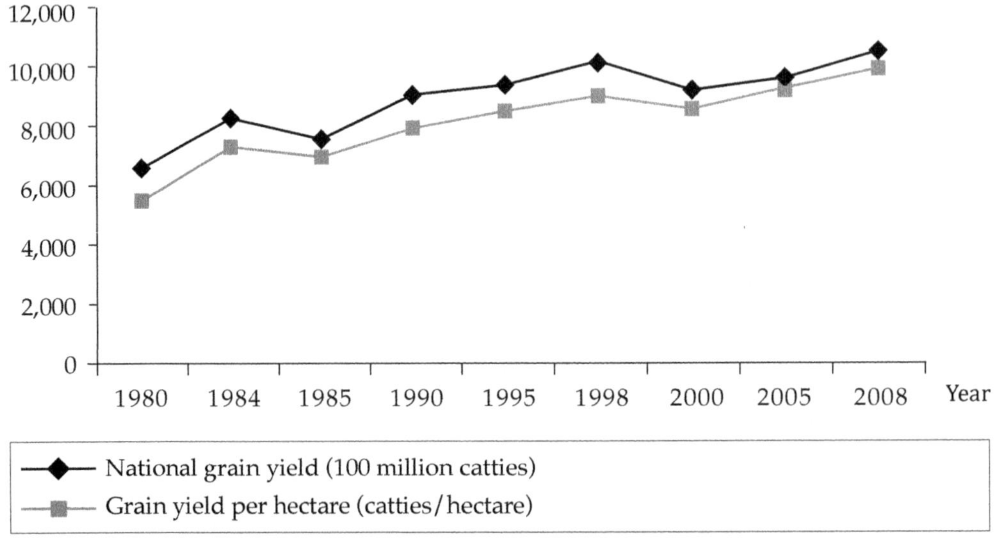

Source: Ministry of Agriculture of the People's Republic of China, *Agricultural Statistics of the People's Republic of China, 1949–2008.*

greater autonomy in agricultural operation, but also better access to the market, which help raise their income. Despite the gap in urban-rural income growth, farmers' income has been impressively elevated as compared to the past. Therefore, the opening and development of rural markets have proved to be beneficial to farmers and villages. Despite the fact that open markers did facilitate the outflow of rural laborers, the massive labor migration has not impede grain production and agricultural production as a whole; and instead, it constitutes a major source of income growth for rural residents.

Summary and Discussions

The sixty-year course of China's rural development is a story of both success and failure, and of both progress and delay. From a sociological perspective, that is, from a viewpoint of structure and transitions, China's rural development can be summarized as follows:

- During the first 30 years of the Reform and Opening Up era, rural life and agricultural production had seen both good and tough times. The agricultural operation system, which not only equalizes land-use rights among rural households but maintains farmers' autonomy in operation, has worked in meeting farmers' basic needs for living and development. On the other hand, agricultural collectivization, which was promoted in a way of political movements, could turn out to harm the enthusiasm of farmers for farming and, adversely, impact the rural economy. This failure indicates that collective operation system is not always effective in promoting cooperation and boosting productivity.
- During the second 30-year period of the Reform and Opening Up era, China had basically pulled its rural residents out of destitution. But rural development were still stuck in certain structural dilemmas, such as the difficulties in constantly raising farmers' income and maintaining sustainable development, the challenge to extricate rural society from backwardness, and the ever widening gap between urban and rural development. On the one hand, rural reforms have freed rural labor from the collective, that is to say, farmers are allowed to take up non-farm jobs. The reforms, on the other hand, should account for the relatively lagging development of rural areas. Although farmers have been allowed to part with their land for capital, they are still rejected by the entrenched system of urban-rural dual structure. Therefore, rural reforms should go further than just detaching rural labor from land. It is necessary to break the old system which prevents

rural laborers from entering non-agricultural industries, and render rural migrants the liberty and better access to the fields of production and life of their own choices.

- Ever since the birth of new China, what has been at the heart of rural reform and rural construction is the relationship between the state and rural households, rather than that between the state and farmers (as suggested by Western scholars). Farmers, as a kind of occupation, are of high homogeneity, while rural households, as a sophisticated complex, are of considerable heterogeneity. Therefore, it is relatively easy to balance the state-farmer relationship. The relationship between the state and rural households, however, is too complicated to handle with a unified set of solutions. This explains the constant failures in China's attempts to reform the scattered small-peasant operation with a unified method. Neither agricultural cooperatives nor people's communes have truly solved the problem in collective operation for that they have both neglected the fact that their participants are not only farmers but also rural households. Thus, it is clearly irrational to pin all hopes of building a new socialist countryside on cooperative organizations, such as agricultural cooperatives.[29] Rural development is more than economic, political and institutional construction, and it is a complex social system project, which requires consideration from the perspectives of systematology and synthesis.
- The damages caused by the people's commune campaign prove that it is dangerous to solely rely on a certain kind of ownership or operation system. The achievements of development are a result of joint effects of multiple factors. The superiority of people's communes, which are large in size and have a high degree of public ownership, though well based in theory, may turn out to be ineffective in China's rural practice. Similarly, the idea that farmland privatization could solve all rural problems, which is held by scholars under the influence of the property rights school of the Western economics, may also prove to be an illusion. The core of the rural land system lies not in the nature of ownership, but in the questions as to how to effectively allocate land to ensure efficient coordination between land and other means of production, such as labor, capital, and technologies, and how to help farmers make more money out of farmland. What is more, even if the land ownership problem is properly settled, it does not mean other problems related to the three rural issues will come to an end accordingly. Holding high expectations on any single kind of solution may end up in the traps of fantasies, just like in the cases of agricultural collectivization and the people's commune campaign.

13

Chapter

Market Transition and Changes in Rural Class Structure

Social classes embody the actual situation and characteristics of social structure. Class analysis is a tradition for Marxist sociologists to investigate and research society, for "in Marxism the division of society into classes is determined by position within the process of production."[1] Status differences in social production and life constitute the basis of social stratification. The mastery of this fact is one of the critical channels for sociologists to know and understand the social structure and its law of motion. Neo-Marxism borrows the strategy of class analysis from Marxist sociology and tries to reveal the contents of class from two different angles: class consciousness and class-induced effects. Then, it works to guide empirical studies to figure out the actual status and influencing factors of class relations and explore possible intervention measures.[2]

An increasing number of Chinese scholars studying contemporary China's social structure and its changes tend now to use class analysis to investigate social stratification, social mobility, and their influencing mechanisms. Some, perhaps out of historical or ideological considerations, disagree with the approach of using class analysis to study Chinese society.[3] Still, as a crucial component of Marxist theory, class analysis remains a useful angle to understand society, even if class struggle is no longer relevant today; it would be a denial of reality to intentionally avoid the discussion or analysis of class. If sociology can objectively uncover the structural characteristics of Chinese classes and make constructive suggestions regarding the strategic policies for regulating class relations, it will greatly contribute to promoting social harmony and stability.

This chapter will discuss, using the method of class analysis, how China's rural class structure has changed since the founding of PRC, how these changes came about, and how they contributed to the China's development.

Social Stratification and Equalization

In the early years of new China, a new rural social structure was taking shape, and at the same time, rural society stepped into a phase of rapid structural transformation. The successful establishment of the new regime was inseparable from the rural structural changes induced by rural reforms advocated by the Communist Party of China (CPC). Those reform campaigns, such as land reforms, rent and interest cuts, and the struggle against local tyrants and evil gentry, found wide support from rural residents who had been deeply troubled by the old class structure.

In the 1930s and 1940s, a huge class difference existed between the privileged and poor peasants with a growing number of peasants being unable to sustain themselves. As commented by Fei after his field study on country life in Wujiang

County, Jiangsu province in the 1930s, "the essential problem in Chinese villages, putting it in the simplest terms, is that the income of the villagers has been reduced to such an extent that it is not sufficient even to meet the expenditure in securing the minimum requirements of livelihood. It is the hunger of the people that is the real issue in China."[4] The problem of absolute poverty was generated from the then class structure, and the privileged classes, such as landlords, loan sharks, tax collectors, dragging villagers down the drain of poverty. An increasing number of peasants recorded a negative net income due to high rents, interest and taxes. According to the data collected by the South Manchuria Railway Company, in a natural village in North China in 1937, one in four middle-peasant households and five in five poor-peasant households had a negative net profit, whereas landlords and rich peasants all reaped a positive profit.[5] To maintain agricultural production, peasants had no choice but to take loans from loan sharks, making them get knee-deep in debt and end up selling land and property. This vicious cycle rendered poor peasants stuck in destitution and even starvation. This can be seen from the rules specified by loan sharks in Shanxi Province:

- Borrower(s) can only get 80% of the amount written in the loan receipt;
- Compound interest method is employed with monthly interest of 3%;
- Loan term is fixed at three months;
- Principal and interest must be repaid in full once the loan comes due;
- Guarantor(s) has the right to sell the property of the borrower(s) upon his failure to pay the debt.[6]

In this way, the privileged and wealthy has milked the hard-earned money from poor peasants. Clearly, this kind of class relation was adversarial and confrontational, and the class structure built upon such a relation was imbalanced and unstable. Thus, it is no wonder that this class structure was later shattered by the communist revolution and a new rural class structure started to arise along with a new set of class relations.

Land reform

Land reform constitutes the basis for the formation of the new rural class structure. During the socialist revolution prior to the founding of new China, land reform has completely changed the social relations and the class structure in old liberated areas. After the reform, privileged classes (such as landlords, rich peasants, local tyrants and evil gentry, and some influential religious groups) were no longer the upper stratum. Instead, they were reduced to ordinary villagers, only with a lower political status, if considering the fact that they were the targets to be fought against in the socialist revolution.

Shortly after the birth of PRC, the socialist transformation of agriculture furthered the land reform in the old liberated areas. Starting from 1950, land reform was implemented step by step in each new liberated area. By 1952, two years after China issued the *Agrarian Reform Law of the People's Republic of China* (hereinafter referred to as the *Agrarian Reform Law*), villages of new liberated areas (excluding minority groups) had basically completed the goals of land reform and successfully equalized the allocation of farmland among all rural classes (including landlords and rich peasants).

In the course of overthrowing the old land system, rural reforms drew on the strategy of dividing classes. As early as the land reform movement in old liberated areas, this strategy had also been applied to reach the effect of "drawing on the plentiful to make up for the scarce, and drawing on the fat to make up for the lean." Take the case of Shilidian Village, for example. Work teams divided rural households into various classes based on the size of land and household economic situation. Those labelled as poor or middle peasants were to be united, while those identified as landlords or rich peasants were to be fought against.[7]

The method of social stratification was not only a heritage from the Chinese socialist revolution, but also an answer to the complexity of land reform. Distinct from general reform, which only touches upon general interests, land reform is directly related to the redistribution of the fundamental interests of people. As required by the *Agrarian Reform Law*, land and other means of agricultural production in the possession of landlords, rich peasants, and other rural groups shall be redistributed to poor and lower-middle peasants. In this sense, land reform is a continuation of the socialist revolution in both economic and social spheres. As being a revolution in nature, land reform must have clearly defined targets, and in order to achieve a better result, it is necessary to make use of political approaches.

Although social stratification was only a reflection of social relations and the class structure, it was widely promoted in rural areas for being recognized as a political approach of land reform. Putting villagers under different classes has a two-fold meaning: First, it is an act to understand and define the existing rural social structure; and second, it is regarded as the basis on which a new social structure and class relations can be developed. Then, each kind of class identity will be assigned an ideological meaning that defines its holder's position in the land reform. This position decides whether a peasant will be a pushing force or a target of a revolution. In the time of peaceful development, such a classification method will be even more effective in telling friends from enemies.

In this land reform, social stratification was also associated with the allocation of resources, in addition to its connection with a person's social status. The most obvious change brought about by this class division was that land lords and rich peasants were downgraded from the upper class to the lower class, and what is more, their social reputations, whether as an individual or a household, were crushed for being the target of political struggle. Poor peasants and hired farmhands, on the other hand, have seen their economic, social and political situations dramatically improved: They not only received a fair share of farmland, but also became the backbone of political revolution and social development. Middle peasants also have their political status raised, though without a big rise in their farmland size.

The new rural land system promoted in early new China has reshaped the social structure by replacing the polarized social class structure with a relatively equalized one. This equalization in the social structure is most notable in the following three aspects:

1. Rural land resources and other property were equally distributed among all classes. The privileged class (including landlords and rich peasants) had their land and other property confiscated, yet during the redistribution, they were still able to receive an equal share the same as those of middle and poor peasants. That is to say, both the allocation of economic resources and the distribution of wealth were equalized in the post-land reform villages.
2. The rural majority has benefited from the reform. The lower-middle and poor peasants not only received farmland and means of production, but also enjoyed a significant rise in their economic, political and social status.
3. The new land system laid an institutional foundation for implementing the principle of distribution according to work (*an lao fenpei* 按劳分配). The land reform has changed the distribution system that allowed landlords and rich peasants to take over the fruits of others' work by taking possession of farmland and capital. Under the new land system, people of every class must work to make a living, thus forming an equalized environment.

Agricultural collectivization

The campaign of agricultural collectivization followed the land reform as the second step of socialist transformation. Starting from the early 1950s, the agricultural collectivization campaign has grouped individual rural households first into mutual-aid teams, then into primary cooperatives, and then into advanced cooperatives, for the purpose of raising agriculture efficiency. In theory, cooperative work should be more efficient than individual labor; yet this is only true under two conditions: First, members have complete autonomy in joining and quitting the cooperative; and second, the management of cooperative organizations must be efficient.

Agricultural collectivization was implemented in a top-down manner, irrespective of individual household's will. Rural households were forced to join the collectives by means of political approaches and ideological propaganda. Take, for example, the case of Fengyang County, Anhui Province. Local villagers who refused to join advanced cooperatives would be labelled as "unenlightened women with bound feet," "capitalist roaders," or "drags on socialist construction." Accordingly, some households would even choose to damage their means of production, such as killing their farming cattle, when they were unwilling to contribute their farmland and means of production for cooperative use.[8]

That said, this campaign proved to be effective in reshaping the class structure of rural society. At the beginning, in fact, rural collectives were established on the basis of voluntary participation. After 1955, however, it became a political obligation for rural households to establish and join cooperatives. Thus, this institutional transformation was an imposed institutional change. The shift in the cooperative method also brought about a new look to the rural social structure. With all rural households joining the cooperatives, the originally independent, separate households were united in groups, which indicated that class differences were minimized and rural residents became equal in status.

Moreover, since rural households have all handed in their means of production to their collectives and worked under cooperation, the disparity between fellow villagers was narrowed to near absolute equalitarianism. In the distribution of collective income, work points and household size respectively accounted for 60% and 40% of a household's income. Considering the fact that farmland was equally distributed according to population, this distribution method, in fact, followed the principle of egalitarian distribution based on population size, though labor work seemed to weigh heavier in calculation.

Agricultural collectivization has eliminated class disparity within each village, so peasants of the same village have become, in a large sense, equal. Rural social disparity existed only between cadres and the masses and between different regions. However, an equalized rural class structure does not necessarily mean equilibrium and stable social relations. This is because the collectivization movement has created two potential problems: First, it has suppressed the effective use of human capital and working enthusiasm of individual rural households; and second, since the cooperation was imposed on rural households by political means, there was a strong tendency of uncooperativeness in agricultural cooperatives. Therefore, the seemingly equal and balanced rural class structure was, in fact, built upon severe economic imbalance, for such social equalization was achieved at the expense of stifling economic vitality and reducing efficiency.

People's commune

In 1958, China started the people's commune campaign under the influence of the ideology which advocated building organizations characterized as being large in size and collective in nature. As a result, advanced cooperatives were restructured in people's communes in the hope of jumping into communism in one step.

The establishment of people's commune system indicated that the socialist transformation of agriculture has basically been completed. Thanks to this campaign, means of production are now brought under collective ownership, farmland is taken away from the possession of individuals, and individual peasants no longer have the rights to occupy and dispose of land. In this sense, the transition to the people's commune system is also a revolution to the property right system, and the collective property right system has been formally established in rural China.

As a new set of institutional arrangements, the people's commune system has an all-round impact on rural development. It has reshaped the mode of economic production, the rural political system, social relations, as well as the rural class structure.

Economically, the people's commune system has implemented a three-level collective ownership. Under such a system, means of production and products of labor were owned by three-level collectives, that is, communes, production brigades, and production teams, among which the production team was considered the basic accounting unit (*sanji suoyou, dui wei jichu* 三級所有，隊為基礎). Collective income was distributed according to each member's contribution. Moreover, to make sure that everybody took part in collective production, individual operations of rural households were strictly limited or even banned. In this way, rural households had to live upon the money and food distributed by the collective, apart from a small piece of land for them to farm on. Therefore, it can be said that in the time of people's communes, class differences did not exist in economic terms. Despite the fact that living conditions did differ from household to household, this was a result of the difference in the ratio of household labor force to family size. Households with ample labor force and few dependents can get a larger share of income and food from the collective, thus enjoying a better life; households with few laborers but many dependents, on the other hand, can only get a smaller share, which makes it difficult to live on.

Politically, the people's commune is a grassroots administrative organ which manages local political, economic, social, and cultural issues in rural areas. With the people's commune becoming the center of rural power, its authorities took charge of every aspect of commune's affairs. Production brigades undertook the function of production accounting, thereby an important management unit. Production teams, on the other hand, only had unofficial management power. Cadres of the two levels of organizations were usually recommended by their fellow team members, and they were responsible for organizing production as well as distributing means of production. In this sense, there were no real elites in the time of the people's commune system. Even though the cadres had certain authority, their power was still restricted by the communes and their fellow team members. For this reason, they did not evolve into the privileged, and more importantly, the status of their families did not rise in the social ladder because of their cadre titles.

Socially, with the implementation of the people's commune system, collectives played a role of organizing peasants and managing rural social affairs. In terms of distributing resources and benefits, there were three pairs of relations: peasant-collective relation, peasant-nation relation, and collective-nation relation. The distribution of collective income was conducted according to the size of each household and the amount of labor each household had put in in collective production. Even for rural cadres, their remunerations were decided on the basis of work points. In this way, the people's commune system has eliminated the class difference among peasants, and there was a strong equalitarian tendency in rural areas.

Agricultural collectivization and the people's commune system have reshaped social relations and the class structure of rural society. Class disparity has been eliminated and peasants have all become equal because of the implementation of collective ownership, collective production, and equal distribution. However, what should not be ignored is that socialist transformation, which is carried out by force through political campaigns, can only get a high level of equality at the expense of peasants' enthusiasm, initiative and creativity, and even economic efficiency. Overall, the non-discriminatory class structure resulting from agricultural collectivization and the people's commune system is inefficient and poverty-inducing.

Social Identity and Equalitarianism

In 1966, the Cultural Revolution was launched. This campaign mainly occurred in urban areas and centered in the fields of culture and political ideology. As a significant historical event and a large-scale political movement, the Culture Revolution has exerted massive impacts on China's social development, social stratification and social mobility.

During the Cultural Revolution, the collective economy originated from the people's commune system was further consolidated. The core of the Cultural Revolution lay in the fight between the proletariat and the bourgeoisie and that between socialism and capitalism. In rural areas, peasants must support the people's commune system, otherwise, they would be vilified as "capitalist roaders" or "enemies of the people" (*jieji diren* 階級敵人), who were all targets of class struggle. Under such a political environment, commune members had no choice but to stay put in communes and devote themselves to collective farming. Though lacking enthusiasm and motivation, commune members dare not leave the collective and start individual production. The Cultural Revolution built up a "protective atmosphere" where everyone was compelled to safeguard the collective economy, which greatly reinforced the system of people's commune and collective farming.

Moreover, the Cultural Revolution also advocated the idea of class struggle which greatly reshaped social environment. The denial of individual initiative and wealth by this campaign restricted people from acting on their own initiative to become better-off. Similarly, in villages, members of production teams were banned from conducting their individual operations.

To maintain the collective economy, the people's commune system had to stand against individual operation, for collective farming would not survive if all group members were busy with their own sideline businesses. Thus, only by curbing individual operation, can collective production be sustained. Since individual economic endeavors were banned, there was little income difference among fellow villagers. As a result, China's rural areas became even more non-discriminatory in the time of Cultural Revolution.

If there was still any class difference in rural China during the Cultural Revolution, it could only be in the aspect of political status. At that time, class struggle was established as the dominant ideology, and as a result, the class identity given to each household during the land reform came back to usage. After agricultural collectivization and the people's commune movement, households which were labelled as "landlords" and "rich peasants" were put under great political and social marginalization, despite the fact that their economic situation was reduced to the same level as or even worse than most households. For example, households with an undesirable class background would be excluded from certain political benefits and opportunities of promotion and mobility. At that time, the social class structure was mainly composed of cadres, workers, and peasants. The basic prerequisite for becoming a cadre was being qualified politically, and one's family political background was an important consideration. In addition to that, in the cases of joining the CPC, enlisting in the army, applying for admission to a school, getting a job, and other opportunities of personal mobility which entailed political review, people whose family background was labelled as lower-middle or poor peasants had the upper hand, while those with a landlord or rich-peasant background had little chance of passing the review. Take college admission for example. As college entrance examination was cancelled during the Cultural Revolution, a person had to be recommended to go to a college, and under this recommendation system, students whose family background was anything other than lower-middle and poor peasants, could hardly get recommended.

During the Cultural Revolution when the mainstream ideology stressed socialist equality, there was almost no economical difference between rural residents; politically, however, class difference did become increasingly evident. What is more, this politics- and ideology-induced rural class difference generated a new kind of social difference — identity difference. Specifically, due to the difference in political status, promotion opportunities opened to each household varied considerably, resulting in unequal economic, political, and social reputations.

That coexistence of political hierarchy and economic equalization was the basic feature of rural social stratification in the time of Cultural Revolution. In rural society, a person's individual and household class identities only had political and symbolic meanings, for they represented the past instead of the present situation. Class identity was often used as a symbolic tool in political struggles at the peak of political campaigns. Policy orientation and political propaganda of the Cultural Revolution have, in a sense, strengthened the equal distribution of rural collectivism. There were actually two criteria guiding the distribution of income and food in rural collectives: First, work amount, that is to say, collective rewards which were principally monetary income, would be distributed according to commune members' work points; Second, household size, which means that food and other material rewards would be distributed to each household according to the number of family members. Under this distribution system, class identity did not play an impacting role.

Although class identity had little impact on income distribution, its influence on social reputation was dramatic. An undesirable family class background was often associated with a bad social reputation. In a society where politics came before everything else, the emphasis on class identity affected social value orientation. Thus during this period, people refrained from pursuing economic gains, such as assets and wealth, just to show their high political consciousness. The same is true even in rural areas. As the pursuit of wealth and economic benefits was against the mainstream value, collectivism and equalitarianism were what advocated by the core social value.

The rural collective distribution system has built a highly equal class structure, which was reinforced and safeguarded by the equalitarianism-praising political ideology. Yet, this was at the expense of peasants' freedom to choose their career or conduct individual operation, and even sacrificed economic efficiency. Just like what Arther Okun has said, "the conflict between equality and economic efficiency is inescapable," and the rural collective system can guarantee equal relations between collective members and between households, but not high economic efficiency; therefore, what we could do is "to put some rationality into equality and some humanity into efficiency."[9]

When used excessively, political approaches would stir up more and more irrationality in the newly developed system. For example, people would be deprived of development opportunities or denounced publicly simply because of an unpopular class identity of their family, or may be targeted as political enemies for making a statement outside the mainstream politics. As evidence by the above examples, it is clear that a heated and irrational social craze was the undertone of the seemingly highly equal social relations. People acted against their rational choices. On the one hand, people seemed timid under the political oppression, but on the other hand, they would actively participate in political struggles impelled by irrational sentiments. In an irrational society, the rise of economic efficiency is almost impossible to come by. The class struggle in rural China was less severe than in cities, yet rural economic efficiency was nevertheless damaged by political fights and interference. With political campaigns being excessively "embedded" into economic activities, the balance of rural society was broken and the tension between villages grew more intense, and thus peasants' enthusiasm for cooperation and production was dented. This was one of the major causes for the inefficient rural collective economy.[10]

Therefore, China's pursuit of an equal society during the Cultural Revolution was in fact a kind of irrational equality. Because it was achieved at the huge cost of economic and social efficiency. This inefficient equalization could have been be avoided if peasants' free will had been respected and the actual rural situation had been taken into consideration.

Rural Reforms and Class Restructuring

The transformation from the collective economy to the household responsibility system has changed not only the operation and management systems of agricultural production, but also the class structure of the rural society. As individual operation had broken off the equalitarian relations in collective farming, rural households which managed to fully apply their human capital were the first to become rich through their talent and hard work. These households, collectively known as the "early-prosperous class" (*xian fu jieceng* 先富階層), were mainly composed of specialized farming operators, specialized animal breeders, self-employed entrepreneurs, owners of township enterprises, and contractors. Compared to ordinary households, the early-prosperous class was economically better off, and this wealth gap was caused by the difference in household human capital. With a piece of contracted land from the collective, rural households were responsible for making their own decisions in agricultural production and their income was mostly a result of their own doings. In this regard, the income difference among rural households would not stir up conflicts.

What created the early-prosperous class and the income difference among rural households was the fact that the household responsibility system had freed rural labor from collective farming, which stimulated the vitality of human capital and the innovation capacity of individual households. This, added with the direct incentive from the fruits of household labor, greatly motivated peasants to devote themselves to agricultural production. All the above factors have contributed to the soaring of agricultural efficiency.

In addition to the above economic influences, this rural economic reform also impacted the economy-politics relation. The dissolution of the rural collective system was accompanied by the declining of political impacts on the collective economy as well as the alteration of national priority — from class struggle to economic development. The shift of social focus was the major driving force behind the reform of the rural social structure. With every household being busy with their own businesses, an income gap emerged among rural households due to the difference in the means of production and the operation style.

The mid-1980s saw the springing up of township enterprises, which initiated the upsurge of China's rural industrialization. In Jiangsu and Zhejiang provinces, the rural industry started up with privately contracted enterprises, which were transformed from commune- or brigade-run enterprises left over from the rural collectives, and then, an increasing number of peasants began engaging in the rural industry by running their own businesses. The rapid industrialization pressed the economic structures of some villages to gradually change from being agriculture-dominated into industry- or non-agriculture–dominated. The transformation of economic structure would inevitably bring about changes in the rural class structure. The most striking one was the emergence of two new economic classes — private entrepreneurs and peasant workers.

Rural entrepreneurs have been constantly growing with the rise of private industrial and commercial enterprises, and they collectively constituted the elite class or the "early-prosperous class" in the rural society. This group of people made far more money than ordinary farmers, and some even beat urban worker and other salary earners.

What came along with the class of rural entrepreneurs was that of peasant workers. In the mid-1980s, a great deal of rural labor either undertook non-agricultural jobs or migrated into urban areas for higher income, and this should give credit to the rapid development of the rural industry and urban non-public sectors which provided rural surplus labor with the chance to move away from agricultural production and rural areas. The out-flown rural laborers made up a new social group — peasant workers. Despite the variations in regions, occupations, life styles, they do share some features which grouped them into the same class. First, they were still registered with a rural *hukou*, even though they had been working non-agricultural jobs in urban areas. Second, since they were mostly hired as contract workers and casual laborers, they were denied full access to health care services, social welfare benefits, and social security when compared to their urban counterparts. Third, their jobs were rather quite unstable and highly mobile. The current *hukou* or household registration system and the labor market system left little chance for peasant workers to become a part of urban society, while placing less control over these outsiders, and therefore rural migrants tended to be highly mobile between regions and jobs.

China has over 200 million rural migrant workers so far, and this number grows at a speed of 6 to 8 million people each year.[11] This rapid growth of the peasant worker group has changed not only the rural class structure, but also the Chinese social structure as a whole. Moving between rural and urban areas and being different from both rural farmers and city residents, rural migrant workers constitute the third group of the Chinese society. Since then, China's social structure has changed from dual to trinity.[12] Peasant workers' high mobility has given rise to a "double dual-structure" in China's society and caused the uncertainty of peasant workers about their future, which will impede future rural development.[13]

The massive outflow of rural labor has led to huge social stratification in rural areas. Since more and more rural laborers have left their home town to find a job in cities, the number of empty nest families is on the rise with the vulnerable, mostly, the elderly, women and children being left behind in villages. Moreover, migrant peasant workers are also divided in terms of occupation and social class. Some get nicely settled down in cities with a good job and a decent income, but the majority of them are still stuck between rural and urban lives. They have made a living in cities but are still rejected by the urban system.

Since the Central Committee of the CPC advocated constructing a socialist market system in 1992, the Reform and Opening Up endeavor has been deepened and expanded. Against the backdrop of marketization and urbanization, class stratification in China's rural society becomes more intense. In terms of urban-rural disparity, the income gap tends to be widening instead of narrowing. According to some scholars, there are ten classes in China, among which 55% are farmers or agricultural laborers, constituting the majority of the lower-middle and bottom layers of the class structure.[14] Meanwhile, the worsening class stratification has been very evident even in the rural society itself, which was reflected not only in the income level, but also in occupation as well as the mode of life and production. Currently, a growing number of rural households live upon non-agricultural income, and farming is no longer the sole income source of their lives. Since agricultural production can only generate a low net yield, rural laborers, especially younger ones, choose to leave their farmland and become peasant workers. A new type of social model is thus formed: Young laborers work in cities as peasant workers while their wives, children and the elderly are left behind in villages. This shows that, in normal life, the rural class structure is increasingly populated by the vulnerable demographic. Yet, at the same time, as rural laborers has switched from conducting agricultural to non-agricultural businesses, rural economy and life quality have made great progress, and the number of people living in absolute poverty has been significantly reduced.

In the new rural social structure, class stratification has been widening, yet there is no contradictive, adversarial relationship between different rural classes. This is because that the difference between rural households is the outcome of their own choices and the resulting opportunities. The most pressing problem induced by the structural changes of rural society is the intermittent absence of social life functions, which, put in plain words, refers to the temporary absence of some family functions, such as education and family security, once the young laborers leave home to work in urban areas.

The stratification of rural classes has intensified the already problematic relation between urban and rural classes, although it has not caused sharp conflicts within rural society. For example, without sound coordinating and regulating mechanisms, peasant workers' relationships with urban managerial authorities and urban employers will probably turn contradictive and adversarial, for they are closely related yet asymmetric in power. In the pursuit of a better life or a higher income, rural migrant laborers may suffer from the rejection of the urban system and the exploitation of their urban employers, and this may put the related social classes into contradictory or even adversarial relationships.

Market Transition and Rural Stratification

China's rural class structure has underwent several dramatic transitions over the past 60 years. It transformed from a confrontational and polarized structure in old China to the revolutionary equality in the early years of New China, then to inefficient equalitarianism, and finally to the market-oriented class division.

The new regime of PRC completely crushed the confrontational, polarized rural class structure. The minority group which was the privileged, including landlords and rich peasants, no longer held the majority of farmland, farming tools and wealth; instead, crucial means of production such as farmland were equally distributed among villagers, bringing equality to rural classes and balance to rural social relations. This equalized and balanced structure resulted from the socialist revolution and fundamental changes to the social structure. The new social relations and class structure reallocated and optimized the relation between labor force and means of production, which helped boost productivity and restore the rural economy. Receiving a fair share of land and other means of production, lower-middle and poor peasants felt full of enthusiasm and motivation to devote themselves to agricultural production. Naturally, household financial status will be generally improved as a result, which will in turn push forward the harmonious development of the rural society and economy. Thus it can be said that the rural class structure was fair and efficient before the agricultural collectivization.

After agricultural collectivization, especially the Great Leap Forward movement and the people's commune campaign, the rural class structure gradually shifted towards inefficient equalitarianism. That is to say, socio-economic differences within villages were narrowed substantially and even approached absolute equality. Class difference was only restricted to political standing, and the social and economic conditions of all rural households were highly similar. This equalized class structure was realized by embedding political campaigns into the collective economy. In other words, the government used political and ideological campaigns to restrain individual rural households from making use of their human capital. For example, individual household who conducted production outside the collective would be put under severe criticism and condemned as "capitalism's tails" (*ziben zhuyi de weiba* 資本主義的尾巴). All laborers must obey the rules and follow the arrangements made by the collective, and they were forbidden to undertake any individual operation. To keep all laborers in the collective, it is a must to eliminate or minimize the differences among rural households, which has severely dampened peasants' creativity and enthusiasm, and therefore, damaged economic efficiency.

Since the Reform and Opening Up policy was launched in the 1978, rapid social stratification has replaced the inefficient equalitarianism in rural society. Instead of putting up with poverty, rural households turned to develop the household economy by making the full of their capability and creativity. As a result, economic efficiency and household income were raised across rural China with some rural households even quickly making a fortune. The income gap between rural households has been growing wider and wider, which can be attributed to households' individual production. In other words, the disparity of income is a reflection and result of social stratification. It was the differences in occupation and operation that led to the stratification of income and economic status.

After the implementation of the Reform and Opening Up policy, the transition from a planned to a market economy was the driving force behind rural stratification. China has been experiencing a comprehensive and rapid structural transformation since 1978.[15] Under this background, the structure of rural society has also embraced dramatic changes: Farmers left unified collective farming and started diversified individual operations, rural households' economic statuses began to differ, and the social class structure went into rapid stratification. The market-oriented transformation was a major important impetus for rural social stratification. The market-oriented economy has opened up the once-closed rural society, greatly enhanced social mobility, and increased the frequency of social structural changes. Evidence from empirical studies also shows that the rural social hierarchy has witnessed some structural changes in the 1980s, during which market players arose as a new force in the rural stratification, and among the wealthiest 20%, the majority were business owners and other new wealthy.[16]

The difference in market opportunities accessible to rural laborers is the major cause for rural stratification. When engaging in market activities, rural laborers' industry, occupation, work location, and human capital will all impact their income level and development opportunities. This fact not only suggests that the market can bring out the economic efficiency of rural households, but also indicates that rural stratification is not a result of exploitation, and thus, no class conflicts are induced hereby. Social stratification is, in a sense, a trend of rural development. Through seeking different development opportunities in the market, rural residents can raise economic efficiency and reach for further development in the process of social stratification.

It is worth noting that rural stratification has impaired the integrity of the rural social structure. In the pursuit of further development and higher efficiency, institutional arrangements and public management should take more account of the vulnerable who are left behind in villages, for example, by channeling more money into rural pension funds and protecting the rights of and providing social care to women and children. Efforts in taking more care of the underprivileged are beneficial to the promotion of social equality.

Compared to rural stratification, the urban-rural stratification is much more prominent, and the urban-rural income gap is constantly widening. This can be attributable to the urban-rural dual structure that denies rural migrants equal access to urban social benefits and the unreasonable market distribution mechanism that sets unbalanced return rates of capital and labor. And what behind these influencing factors of the growing urban-rural divide are inharmonious and contradictive social relations. Therefore, to settle the urban-rural stratification seems even more important for maintaining social stability and promoting social development in rural areas.

Summary and Discussions

The rural reform of 1978 serves as a dividing line that splits China's 60-year rural development into two phases. During the first 30 years, the rural class structure has went from social equalization and class identity symbolization via institutional transformation to equalitarianism and class struggle socialization via political movements. In the early years of new China, the new regime crushed the confrontational and polarized class structure though all kinds of rural reforms, such as the land reform. By equally distributing land and other means of production, China significantly raised rural productivity and defused the confrontation between different rural classes. At that time, class identity was merely a political symbol without any practical social meaning.

Agricultural collectivization and the people's commune campaign replaced individual production with the system of collective management by embedding political campaigns into the collective economy. Collective equalitarianism was realized at the expense of economic efficiency. It suppressed individual creativity and undermined human capital by political and ideological means. As a result, the economic gap between different rural households was eliminated, yet class struggle — as an important political approach against social inequality — was embedded in social life, which became a pillar of the inefficient equalitarian structure.

During the second half of China's rural development, rural society has gradually walked out of the plight of inefficient equalitarianism and become increasingly stratified under the impetus of market economic transformation. First, in terms of the income level, some rural households get rich first by applying their household human capital and making use of market opportunities, and these people has formed a new rural class — "early-prosperous class." Second, as rural labor was released from collective farming, many villagers started to leave farmland and their hometowns to work in cities, and as a result, there emerged a new social class with Chinese characteristics and the features of the transitional economy — peasant workers. Moreover, driven by the marker economy, rural laborers are highly mobile in terms of industry, occupation, and work location, which has speeded up rural stratification.

China's rural class structure, whether before or after the 1978 rural reform, has always been relatively balanced and stable. There are no confrontations and conflicts in social relations, and of all times, the only difference in the rural social structure lies in the economic incentive mechanism and economic efficiency. But, what should be noted is that the urban-rural dual structure and the unreasonable distribution mechanism (between capital and labor) have brought new challenges to the urban-rural class structure. Latent conflicts and instability resulting from these challenges are even riskier than rural stratification. Therefore, in the construction of a harmonious society, China should focus on coordinating between urban and rural areas and between capital and labor distribution, and constantly improve the two relationships through reforms, institutional innovations and legislation.

14

Chapter

Post-Earthbound China and Its Development Dilemmas

Upon the research on the ethnography of the Yangtze Valley,[1] Fei pointed out that "Chinese society is fundamentally [earthbound]."[2] Since then, however, China has experienced many major social changes: land reforms, socialist transformation, the people's commune campaign, household responsibility system, construction of new socialist countryside, urbanization, and the like. So, is Fei's observation still pertinent to China's rural areas today? If the answer is no, then what is the fundamental feature of current rural society?

In the presence of marketization and globalization, rural China has gone through great structural changes. Then, what are the structural features of the rapidly-transforming rural China? If "earthbound" is no longer a right term describing the nature and trend of rural development, then, is "post-earthbound" a better fit to the current rural social structure which is going through huge changes?[3]

In this chapter, we will first review how the earthbound theory explains the social structure of grassroots rural China in the first half of the 20th century; and then, from a post-earthbound perspective and practical experience, we will try to summarize the nature and features of the rapidly-transforming rural society.

The Coming of Post-Earthbound China

Earthbound China

"Chinese society is fundamentally [earthbound.]"[4] — this is an incisive statement made by Fei on the nature of China's rural society. He came to this conclusion upon his field study and his research upon the local ethnography of a village, Kaihsienkung, in Wujiang County, Jiangsu Province.

Fei explained Chinese society's "earthbound" nature from the following three aspects:

- "Soiled" country people
- Low mobility and parochialism
- A familiar society

"Soiled" country people

In the Chinese language, the term *xiangtu* 鄉土 (earthbound) is made up by *xiangxia* 鄉下 (countryside) and *tuqi* 土氣 (soiled). Although the label *tuqi* may seem pejorative, or to say, judgmental, it is appropriately used here. As Fei has put it, "Country people cannot do without the soil because their very livelihood is based upon it."[5]

In China's traditional rural society, peasants lived in the countryside, which was not only in the sense of ecological and geographical space, but also in terms of social-spatial hierarchy. "City" is the opposite of "countryside," but the meaning of "city" used in the present day is slightly different from it was in the past. Today, city residents are mostly working non-agricultural jobs and governmental jobs. That is to say, today, the major difference between "countryside" and "city" dwellers is mostly occupational or occupation-related rather than social-hierarchical. In contrast, the difference in the past is in social status. In the traditional society, cities were where the ruling class, upper class, social elites and a small number of underclass people who worked to serve the privileged lived. Therefore, living in cities indicated a higher social status, while living in the countryside a lower one.

Being "soiled" is a major feature of traditional villages and their people. The majority of rural residents work as peasants to make a living. They depend on farming for means of livelihood, and in turn, they have grown to have an earthy character. Throughout the history of China, generations of peasants have been longing for owning their own piece of farmland. Farmland, naturally, is the core of rural issues.

The Chinese history has seen many dynasties severely weakened or even overthrown by peasant revolts, and the trigger of almost every revolt is farmland related. For example, the Taiping Rebellion raised the slogan of "equally sharing farmland, food, clothing and money" (*you tian tong geng, you fan tong shi, you yi tong chuan, you qian tong shi* 有田同耕，有飯同食，有衣同穿，有錢同使), and the socialist revolution conducted by the CPC called on peasants to "divide the farmland of local tyrants" (*da tuhao, fen tiandi* 打土豪，分田地). In this sense, land can be the best incentive to motivate peasants. The unfairness of land distribution is probably the most sensitive issue in rural society, which can lead to the most serious problem. Once the allocation of farmland goes wrong or turns out to be severely unfair, social tensions would be intensified and may even trigger a conflict or revolution.

Low mobility and parochialism

In China's country side, "the majority of farmers live grouped together in villages"; by contrast, "in rural areas of the United States, each family is geographically separated from its neighbors and constitutes its own individual collectivity."[6] Moreover, although both rural and urban residents live in groups in China, their states of living are quite different. From the perspective of social transitions, social mobility is what makes towns and cities. In other words, towns and cities come into being when people gather around in the same place. The high level of division of labor and cooperation is the reason why urban residents would like to live in neighborhoods.

On the other hand, "it is normal for farmers to settle in one spot for generations."[7] This indicates that China's traditional rural society is closed and lack of mobility. Most villagers are born into instead of moving into a village, where they depend on farming for a living. "The division of labor required for agriculture is very simple,"[8] mostly within the scope of household or based on gender. Households' production can basically guarantee rural residents' self-sufficiency in food supplies, and specialized division of labor is not necessary. According to Fei, peasants tend to live in villages out of four reasons:

> (1) The piece of land that each family cultivates is invariably small. This is a petty agricultural economy; people live together in the same place so that they can be close to their fields.
> (2) Where irrigation is required, people must work together as a group, so living together is quite convenient.
> (3) Living together as a group also greatly contributes to everyone's security.
> (4) We practice partible inheritance of land, which gives an equal share of an estate to all male heirs. Therefore, because of this practice of dividing land among brothers, and thus attaching each of them to the same soil, over a period of several generations small communities grow into large villages.[9]

Village is not only the form of existence of China's rural society, but also the basis of rural social relations and systems. The British anthropologist Feuchtwang stated upon his research of Chinese villages:

> A traditional place, including a so-called natural village or hamlet (*ziran cun* 自然村), is, in short, a ritual and historical unit whose residents are divisible into those who claim descent from an original settlement, however resent it was in fact, and those who were later immigrants. It is common property in being a shared environment and a shared destiny which can be remedies by cosmogonic ritual adjustment or by *fengshui* treatment.[10]

When living in the same village, people will grow into sharing a sense of identity which works as ties binding villagers in the same group together and making villagers feel that the village is their shared environment.

The low level of mobility intensifies the exclusiveness of internal relations and activities within a village, which contributes to the parochialism in social relations and culture of each village. This parochialism is established collectively by people who live there and are not likely to migrate. In each village, the relationship among fellow villagers, as well as the knowledge, custom, rules, and systems formed during social interactions are unique in its own way. Therefore, it is safe to say that villages in earthbound China are homogenous inside, while parochial or heterogeneous outside.

"It is a different village five *li* (2.5 kilometers) away, a different set of customs ten *li* (5 kilometers) away" is a well-known Chinese proverb which right describes the parochial rural culture and regional variations in rural China. In a rural society which is closed and lacks regional interactions, villages are hardly influenced by external factors, and this makes it possible for each village to form their unique characteristics. The parochialism of rural China is closely related to its state of being closed. To say villages are closed does not mean that villages are completely closed to the outside. Instead, it suggests the process of transition from being closed to open.[11]

A familiar society

Village society is made up by people who grow up and live together. The inner relation between fellow villagers, according to E. Durkheim, is a kind of organic solidarity, different from the so-called mechanical solidarity between urban residents. Organic solidarity is developed based on ritual and customs, while mechanical solidarity arises from the complex division of labor.

Village society is a familiar society, which means that all members of this society are familiar with each other. Here, familiarity has a three-fold meaning:

- Fellow villagers have grown quite familiar with each other from their frequent interactions. Living in the same village, villagers will inevitably have daily contact with each other and develop close relationships. Then, naturally, fellow villagers will develop a shared sense of identity and intimacy, and reach a consensus in action. Villagers generally regard themselves as "a member of a certain village," and therefore, they will act in concert when it comes to their common interests.
- Rural residents are pressured by a shared set of ethics to save their "faces" (*mianzi*, reputation). Living in a society where almost everyone else is your acquaintance, one is always bound by the top rule of saving his own face. Whatever a person does in whatever context, he must take care of his and other people's faces. The reason why there is strong trust among fellow villagers is not simply because they know each other, but because they are under the pressure to save their faces. Here, face serves as a guarantee in daily interactions. Face has a two-fold meaning: first, a kind of moral

and ethical responsibility developed based on intimate feelings between acquaintances, usually between neighbors, friends, and relatives; and second, the public morals and ethical responsibilities formed by living as a community. Being called as *diu lian* 丢臉 (losing face) and *buyao lian* 不要臉 (shameless) is considered serious accusations for breaking public behavior rules in a familiar society. The reason why fellow villagers feel the need to keep their "faces" is that they share the same set of moral standards. In villages, familiarity is precisely what compels fellow villagers to obey the ethical constraints and moral norms. If a member of the familiar society breaks the rule, by acting against the custom or committing theft, for example, this person will be despised and condemned by the public. Saving one's face is, in a sense, the basic requirement for being a social person. Therefore, for the sake of saving their faces, villagers act cooperatively. This is what brings the familiar society mutual understanding and trust.

- Primary social relations have been developed between fellow villagers. In a familiar society, people not only know each other, but also have overall mastery of each other's family background and social relations. Therefore, in this sense, a familiar relationship is not merely a relational pattern between individuals, but more of a kind of primary social relations.

To interpret rural society as a semi-familiar society is,[12] in a sense, a misunderstanding of the familiar society, or an understanding of the rural structure and evolution from a modern perspective. Familiarity in a familiar society does not mean that people know each other well, and therefore cannot be measured by modern criteria such as the degree of intimacy and the frequency of interactions. In this sense, there is no such thing as semi-familiar society. We can only judge whether a society is a familiar society or a stranger society, but not how much "familiarity" there is. It is impossible to make this kind of judgement without quantitative empirical analysis. As for the degree of influence of familiarity has in a society, the research into social network by measuring the intensity and extent of individual's social network[13] can shed some light upon how much influence social connections have in society, and how rural residents of the present time interact and communicate with each other.

The difference between a familiar society and a stranger society lies in the macrostructure and nature of the society, rather than how well each person knows one another at the micro level. There are acquaintances and strangers in both stranger and familiar societies. It is difficult to decide how many percent of acquaintances in the entire population could make a society a familiar society, and how many a stranger society. Similarly, for individuals, how well do they know each other could make them acquaintances? Obviously, we should define a familiar relationship based on its nature, not the level of intimacy.

It is accurate and profound for Fei to summarize grassroots Chinese society as an earthbound society. His theory of earthbound China is still up there among the most important perspectives in the research of traditional and modern rural society. It is also worth noting that the earthbound society has undergone great changes in the presence of modernization, urbanization, and globalization. This may herald a new era of post-earthbound China.[14]

Post-earthbound China

While the earthbound rural structure is still in effect, modernization has shadowed its effects on all facets of China — economically, politically, and culturally, which gives earthbound China a tint of modernity and ushers in the age of post-earthbound society. In other words, post-earthbound society is where the residential pattern is still earthbound, while the socioeconomic structure and people's spirits are a mixture of earthboundness and modernity. Villages remain the basic form of rural social organization and are still the opposite form of cities, which means that there are no substantial changes in the residential structure. Residents of villages, however, have changed greatly. Social stratification among villagers in some villages has become quite intense. Agricultural production has changed from being the sole source of livelihood into just a part of many occupations that rural residents take up. Increasingly more villagers have begun getting involved in various kinds of non-agricultural businesses alongside farming. In this sense, the trend of occupational stratification and mobility is quite evident in rural China.

What is more notable is that with the massive outflow of rural labor, villagers have become widely aware of and even welcome modern values and ideas. The state of mind of rural residents, especially that of the new generation of farmers, has changed dramatically. Modern villages are no longer what they were in the past, for despite a same residential structure, the look of villages and the spirit of rural dwellers have changed massively.

The transformation from earthbound to post-earthbound rural society is mainly reflected in the following aspects:

- More and more villagers become modern and are no longer "soiled."
- Villages enter in a period of great mobility and intense transition and stop being closed and immobile.
- The social network of the familiar society further expands.

Modern instead of "soiled"

Agriculture production has changed from being the sole source of livelihood into just one part of household income. Without the support of off-farm income, farmers will probably have no enough money to purchase means of production to sustain agricultural production. Thus, even the most conservative farmers would do more than just farming and hope to make higher profits from the market.

Since agricultural production can only yield low marginal income, a growing number of rural households have built their livelihood upon non-agricultural, non-rural income. As a result, massive rural laborers flood into cities where they work in commercial and service industries. Hardly anybody born later than the 1970s would like to stay in villages and do farming jobs. The only "soiled" villagers, nowadays, are probably the elderly, married women, and underage children who are left behind in rural areas by migrant workers. This is because the elderly are not suitable for frequent migration considering their age, and married women have to stay in villages to take care of their homes and children. Children are usually left behind in villages out of consideration for the high living cost in cities and the fact that migrant workers are fully occupied by their urban jobs and have no time to look after their children.

Migrant workers are increasingly less inclined to do farming. In the past, they would come back to villages during the sowing season and again at harvest time, resting daily field management upon their left-behind family members. Now, many migrant workers decide to drop out of farming in view of the low agricultural income and high travelling expenses and income losses for absence from work. Farm work is mostly left to their old-aged parents and left-behind wives, and now farming is just for the purpose of self-sufficiency. Generally, it is not common for fellow villagers to farm other people's land, unless they are close relatives. The two sides will negotiate beforehand, and then the land owner will set aside the piece of uncultivated land they both agree on for the fellow villager to grow, while in return, the villager will pay corresponding agricultural taxes for the land owner. After agricultural taxes have been abolished in 2006, however, more land was left untilled. This is because when one's land is contracted to his fellow villager, the land owner would expect the villager to give something back in return, yet the villager may think that the land would otherwise be unprofitable but for his work, and thus he does not want to share his fruits of labor with the land owner. As a result, the amount of uncultivated farmland grows rapidly in the presence of unclear responsibilities and duties of contracted land. At present, the circulation of farmland still happens mostly between close relatives, and the land of many rural migrants are left uncultivated.

The fact that many farmland are left untilled reveals that farmers have become less attached to land as they used to be; instead, they now have an increasingly strong desire to shake off the shackles of land. According to the author's investigation in Xiaogang Village, Fengyang County, many rural households were eager to transfer their contracted land for cash at the price of CNY7,000 per *mu*, because it is better to hold cash as whether the land contract can be renewed after it is due is still unknown. From the above, it can be seen that rural residents of post-earthbound China are no longer "soiled," but modern and rational.

The market economy has been lessening rural residents' dependence upon farmland and erasing their feature of being "soiled." The new generation of villagers have now grown modern and are gradually getting rid of their rural traits in their interactions with urban life and modern culture.

Mobile and transformational instead of closed and immobile

Villages in the post-earthbound China has swung from one extreme to the other — from being immobile and closed to highly mobile. More and more farmers have left their home villages to pursue non-agricultural jobs in cities and frequently move between different geographical locations, industries, and jobs. The mobility of rural migrant workers is even higher than that of urban residents or people working in public sectors. This is because urban residents tend to move upwards or horizontally for a promotion or a similar-level position, while rural migrant workers move to get new job opportunities. Urban job opportunities are highly uncertain, which makes the movement of farmer-turned workers also uncertain. Therefore, rural migrants' high mobility is connected with high uncertainty.[15] For most rural migrants, their urban job opportunities are got by venturing into the market, thus highly uncertain. So, they have to frequently switch between different cities and jobs. The coexistence of high mobility and high uncertainty is a major structural feature of rural China.

Inside villages, farming households are no longer the dominant type, and the economic situation is not similar any more for every family. During the rapid social transformation, villages are also experiencing great social stratification. Despite still labeled as being "rural," such as "rural entrepreneurs" and "rural migrants," villagers have become highly divided in terms of social stratum and occupation. They may be owners of private firms, individual entrepreneurs, self-employed individuals or employees of any sector — be it agriculture, industry or services.

Rural social transformation is now mainly driven by the trend of rural residents venturing into the market. As villages have opened themselves up to the outside world, more and more rural households have the chance to seek new development opportunities outside their home villages. These opportunities, unstable and uncertain as they may be, have brought considerable changes to the social, economic and cultural structures of rural society. In addition to that, the opening-up policy is another force behind China's rural transformation. In the earthbound society, the social structure is relatively closed and independent, and without an inside acquaintance, an outsider can hardly blend in. However, the opening-up policy has changed this situation. In this era of modernization, urbanization, and marketization, villages in many places are actively or passively opening their doors to the outside world. Villagers make use of their land resources to seek market opportunities in search of more income. In some villages where local industry and commerce are better developed, for example, people open their land and houses for rent and sale in the market; and some other villages would leverage local cultural and ecological resources to develop tourism. By opening up, rural China has quickly transformed from being earthbound to modern, and traditional villages are directly linked with modern markets and modern culture. Although maintaining the identity as village and inheriting the traditional living pattern as a compact community, many villages have already gone through dramatic social and cultural changes, especially the villages in Jiangsu, Zhejiang, Guangdong, and Fujian provinces and other developed southeastern coastal areas. Villages in these areas have completed industrialization and urbanization despite still being recognized as "village" in administrative division.

Expansion of the familiar society

The post-earthbound China is still a familiar society with the only difference that the familiarity is not restricted to between fellow villagers. The social network of the familiar society has been stretching out along with the increase of social mobility.

For rural migrants, their acquaintances have been expanded from people in their own home village to include those from their nearby villages met in their urban jobs. This constitutes the important basis of rural migrants' social networks in cities.

This broader familiar society is actually built on the basis of the familiarity in the earthbound society, but it goes beyond the border of a village. Different from geographical connections, this expanded social network is associated with the credibility of the post-earthbound villagers. Now, when rural residents migrate to work in cities, they will, via the introduction of a mutual friend, get acquainted with the people who share a similar background from nearby villages. At first, they may not know each other at all, but after the introduction by a fellow villager, they will soon have a thorough knowledge about each other, thereby building a sense of trust between them.

Rural migrants from nearby villages tend to live closely in their migrated cites. In Beijing, for example, there were many famous communities of migrants, such as "Zhejiang Village,"[16] "Henan Village," and "Xinjiang Village." By living near each other, rural migrants can have their social networks further expanded and create new social relationships. This new kind of social networking, like that in the old days, performs the function of providing mutual support and chances of exchanges. What is more, it is also an important social mechanism for rural migrant workers to reconstruct their own social network and adapt to the city life.[17]

In villages, the social network of the familiar society and its corresponding trust system are largely the same. The rural customs such as personal favors and saving "faces" still work in villagers' daily interactions. If there are any differences, it will be the increasingly widespread penetration of market rules in rural activities.

Double-Dual Pattern in China's Rural Society

The transformation from earthbound to post-earthbound rural society also reflects in the changes of rural relations and rural social structure. To explain the social relations of grassroots China, Fei introduced the theory of the "differential mode of association" (*chaxugeju* 差序格局). It refers to not only the structural features of rural society, but also the fundamental characteristics of the cultural-psychological formation of China's traditional culture as well as the grassroots social structure. From the perspective of selfishness, Fei compared China's differential mode of association to that of Western countries.[18] According to him,

> In the pattern of Chinese organization, our social relationships spread out gradually, from individual to individual, resulting in an accumulation of personal connections. These social relationships form a network composed of each individual's personal connections. Therefore, our social morality makes sense only in terms of these personal connections.[19]

Fei summarized the features of China's differential mode of association as follows:

- The differential mode of association is a self-centered social network, which has the characteristics of egocentrism. The basic unit of earthbound society is the social network made of each person's family members and relatives. A person himself is the center of his network. For each network, there is only one center, and thus there are no two same networks considering the fact that no two people in the world could have exactly the same group of relatives.

As there is always a self at the center of each social network, it is egocentrism rather than individualism that constitutes the ideological pillar of the self-centered social network. Western society advocates individualism and stresses the equal status of every individual. In contrast, egocentrism always takes a self as the center, and therefore, it is understandable that "the Chinese would sacrifice their families for their own self-interests, their party for their families' interests, their country for their party's interest, and the whole world for their country's interests."[20] Selfishness is a major social problem of the earthbound society.

- The pattern of Chinese social organization is based on the traditional ethical idea of Confucianism — *renlun*人倫 (human relationships), and it put people in different levels and classes. In Confucianism, *renlun* is the rules guiding the interpersonal interactions. These rules stress differentiation between seniors and juniors, the intimate and the unconnected, the remote and the close, the noble and the base, the superior and the inferior. So it is clear that Confucianism advocates hierarchical differentiations in human relationships. Under such a social structure, a person will develop his own social web with oneself being the frame reference; and for himself, everybody else is of a different hierarchical status.

  In traditional China, the rules of social interactions are called *li* 禮 (etiquette). It requires that one should act differently towards different people according to their social status. For example, how people treat their family members should be different from the way they treat strangers. This shows that the differential mode of association share some features of particularism in interpersonal interactions. In other words, people do not act upon egalitarianism and universalism in the differential mode of association.
- This pattern of organization is also associated with the boundaries between the group and the individual and between others and our own selves, and has the special quality of elasticity. How family, the basic unit of any society, is viewed in the eyes of Chinese people is dramatically different from the way it is viewed by Western people. In the West, family means one's nuclear family that consists of a pair of spouses and their unmarried children. In China, however, the boundary of family is unclear and flexible. A family can be just the nuclear family or the extended one which also includes the

spouses' siblings and parents.

The elasticity of the social network of this pattern is decided by the power and authority of each center. When the central is influential, its social network would expand to a broader scope and receive more recognition from people. But if the central is weak, its social web would be small with less social acceptance. This is why in China, people usually "seek connections in higher places and do things for the sake of friendship."[21]

In terms of cultural-psychological structure, some ideas and principles of the differential mode of association still exist today. For example, people still value personal relations and hierarchical differentiation in their social interactions. In addition to that, the concepts of kindship and family culture are still alive or have been reconstructed a little bit. The ideas of "selfishness", "self" and "hierarchy," however, have been changed under ideological propaganda and political movements. Collectivism and socialism affect, to a certain extent, people's social actions.

In terms of the rural social structure, the kinship network and family influence still play an important role in today's villages. In particular, after the introduction of the Reform and Opening Up policy, family culture and influence have resumed in Southern China.[22] Kinship and clan forces continue to have a strong influence over local elections and public affair management. However, the present relationships and power of clans are quite different from what they were in traditional earthbound society.

The differential mode of association is transforming into a double-dual pattern alongside the social change from earthbound to post earthbound society.

The term "double-dual pattern" refers to the dual system in both the structural and institutional formation of China's rural society. In terms of structural formation, the dual system is reflected in not only political but also economic spheres. Rural political structure is a combination and struggle of traditional and modern power. On the one hand, governmental administrative authorities have embedded their influence into rural society through socialist transformation and political movements, and also legitimized their power through institutionalization. On the other hand, rural elites would fully utilize their clan culture and mobilize their social resources to win themselves a seat in village politics. Therefore, clan culture and family influence are no more than a kind of political tools, and they are no longer the basis of rural politics. After all, because of the regime building and legal construction in grassroots villages, the state, administrative organs, and laws have become the dominant forces in regulating and affecting rural social relations. As for the rural economic structure, post-earthbound rural society still retains the traditional small-peasant economy, and at the same time, villagers have been actively participating in market activities and modern economic sectors. Thus, rural economy is neither completely traditional nor totally modern, and it is in nature a dual economy combining both traditional and modern features.

From the perspective of institutional formation, the dual system is manifested in both the urban-rural dual structure and the public-nonpublic dual structure. Specifically, on the one hand, the transition into the market economy affords rural labor force the chance to migrate into urban areas to undertake non-agricultural jobs, thus greatly raising the mobility of villages. On the other hand, as the urban-rural separation system has excluded these migrant workers from getting jobs "inside the system" (that is, in the public sector), which means that rural migrants only have restricted access to social welfare, their social uncertainty will be increased considerably.[23] In such a way, rural surplus labor has been double rejected by urban-rural and public-nonpublic dual structures.

This double-dual pattern has rendered villagers stuck between rural residents and urban residents, farmers and workers, and therefore, making their cognition and expectation of themselves and the society highly uncertain. This state of uncertainty is completely different from the closed and stable state under the differential mode of association, which exists in the earthbound villages.

Dilemmas in Recent Rural Development

In the process of social development and social transformation, it is unavoidable that people have to choose between old and new conditions, systems, concepts and structures. And making choices may involve dilemmas. Giddens put the dilemmas that trap modern society into five categories: globalization, individualism, left and right in political terms, political agency, and ecological issues.[24] These are dilemmas from a macroscopic, or more specifically, political perspective. Then in this era of modernization, are there certain dilemmas impeding the development of rural China? If there are, what are they?

Rural China is now standing in the crossroads of development. The tides of modernization, urbanization, globalization, and marketization have put rural China in the middle of various kinds of dilemmas. The questions that need to be addressed include: Should social order be maintained by ritual or by law? Should rural areas be self-governing or state-governing? Should rural economy continue rely on agriculture for further development or should it head towards industrialization? Should villages be kept or turned into towns? Should rural laborers stay in villages or migrate into urban areas? These are questions worthy of careful thoughts and proper solutions.

Rule by ritual or by law

Social order refers to the state of society in which people communicate, interact, and cooperate with each other according to a certain set of rules and routines. Social order is what connects people together and is the foundation of daily life. Without normal social order, there will be no social life. To maintain normal social order, it takes a series of rules and the power to ensure the effective implementation of these rules. The regulation or mechanism which keeps society in order is called social control. It is needed in every society to regulate the behaviors of each individual in order to make people's behaviors conform to public standards.

In earthbound rural China, maintaining social order is greatly different from that in modern society. By saying they are different, it does not mean that there was no law or no need of laws in the past. It fact, earthbound society was ruled by rituals.[25]

According to Fei, rituals have the following implications:

- Rituals are publicly recognized behavioral norms that do not require any concrete structure of political power in order to be effective.
- Rituals are accumulated social experience.
- Rituals are tradition that has been formed in societies that do not frequently change.
- Rituals are a habit formed in the process of cultivating oneself. One learns to conform to tradition on one's own initiative.[26]

There is no written law in ritual-ruled earthbound society, that is to say, it do not need an external force to maintain people's behavioral norms. Therefore, in this sense, ruling by rituals is the opposite of ruling by laws. Both ways can achieve an orderly and disciplinary society, just with different approaches. Then, in the absence of law, what was earthbound society like?

In Huang's research of rural disputes in the Qing Dynasty and the Republic of China, he found that during the period of 1750—1900, civil cases took a third of all cases in county courts, and this percentage grew to around 50% in the Republic China era. Most civil suits and disputes involved land ownership, debt collection, marriage, and inheritance.[27] This shows that earthbound China is said to be lawless only in a relative term. Along with the advance of modernization, an increasing number of people in earthbound China turned to the law to solve their disputes. There were three ways to handle civil disputes and maintain social order: informal civil mediation, formal court adjudication, and in between.[28] In a society governed by rituals, social order is formed by ethics, conventions, and traditional authority, while little does it require external, legal, and political forces.

What make it possible for earthbound society to be ruled by rituals is fact that the then society hardly ever changed. As Fei stressed, "A rule of laws and a rule of rituals occur in two different social circumstances.... A society governed by rituals cannot easily appear in an era of rapid changes. But such a system of rule is characteristic of Chinese rural society."[29]

With rapid social transformation, the social circumstance has changed, and rural society which was once low in mobility and high in homogeneity is divided into various strata. Despite the fact that rituals and conventions still impact people's choice of action in certain ways, for example, many farmers would still turn to the traditional or habitual approach to solve their disputes, it is undeniable that administrative and legal approaches are increasingly adopted by rural residents, thanks to the regime construction and legal development in grassroots China.

Therefore, it is inevitable that, in the new phase of rural order development, the country is faced with the dilemma of whether rural society should be ruled by rituals or by laws. On the one hand, the rule of rituals is a tradition of rural China and still has impacts on many issues in post-earthbound society. On the other hand, modern institutions and laws have been constantly stretching into rural social life, and they are being accepted and used by more and more rural residents. In actual practice, these two sets of rules do work together to maintain social order. The coexistence of the both rules may result in two conditions: If they go hand in hand, no choice needs to be made; but if they contradict each other, a dilemma will arise.

In reality, choosing between a rule of law and a rule of rituals is much more difficult than what the theory of legalization has predicated. In theory, a rule of law is certainly a better idea than a rule of rituals. But in practice, such a conclusion cannot be easily drawn. For rural society, laws and legal forces are external power while rituals are gradually developed within society itself. External forces, when being used to solve internal disputes or social problems in a village, may turn out to be highly efficient, but the actual effects and results are often undesirable, and sometimes even counter-effective.

Self-governing or state-governing

Although China's rural society is transitioning to a post-earthbound society and becoming less isolated and more open in the process, villages remain relatively independent communities. Villages are barely connected, and the public sphere in rural communities is still underdeveloped. Under these circumstances, self-governance is necessary in village communities. In modern China, however, rural affairs have been an inseparable part of state affairs, as they are also national issues that carry a wider significance for the development of the entire country.

Rural society is, in fact, caught in a tussle between self-governance and state governance. The state has been trying to organize the structure of rural society into an administrative system and social life into organizations, building a grassroots administration that would centralize the traditionally scattered peasants. During the socialist transformation period, this was manifested in the implementation of the people's commune, which was organized along the levels of production brigades and production teams. After the implementation of the Reform and Opening Up policy, the abolishment of the "People's Commune" and the reestablishment of villages, as well as the implementation of the villagers' self-governance reforms, are all measures aimed at reconstructing a grassroots organization system comprised of townships, administrative villages, and natural villages, such that even though village-level organizations are not considered part of the national administration system, their actual functions do carry administrative features.

The state has further issued the *Organic Law of the Villagers' Committees of the People's Republic of China*, allowing villagers to directly elect the administrative officers of their village. While this law reinforces the legitimacy of the village administration, and it is also an attempt to establish rational legal authority in villages and gain the support of rural society for this system. The control that grassroots authorities have on the operating and distribution rights of collective interests can lead to the development of what Duara characterizes as entrepreneurial brokerage: Under the collective land ownership system, the villagers' committee is virtually the broker or agent handling their rights to the village's collective land. As the impact of urbanization and marketization expands further, some rural communities are seeing increasingly more disputes over the distribution of interests from land expropriation and collective development, and in dealing with these issues, the rationality and impartiality of grassroots authorities are being challenged.

While grassroots authorities have become more democratic and legitimate in their working formalities and procedures, they have grown increasingly distant from both the rural communities and the state administrative system; that is, the grassroots authorities are facing marginalization. This type of authority is no longer viewed as necessary by villagers and its position in the state administrative system appears to be diminishing in importance as well.

In 2006, agricultural taxes were abolished. The grassroots authorities no longer carry the function and responsibility of collecting taxes. Thus, the future of grassroots authorities lies in developing its functions in the administration of rural society or public affairs.

The establishment of village self-governance comes after the implementation of the household responsibility system and the abolishment of the people's commune system, based on the *Organic Law of the Villagers' Committees of the People's Republic of China*. The aim is to have villagers manage their own administration, education, and services, and the grassroots authorities corresponding to this self-governing system are the "Two-Village Level committees": the villagers' committee and the Party's branch committee for the village. The villagers' committee appears to the center of self-government, since its members of this committee are directly elected by the local villagers. But even though the committee's legal status is merely a self-governing organization, in actual practice it acts like a quasi-political organization, as it is in charge of the local collective economy in many places.[30]

As a village-level administrative system, villagers' self-governing exhibits two characteristics: One, it is state-led, and two, its procedures are democratic. The state plays a leading role in establishing a standard form of self-governing organization and a standard system of administration for village-level affairs; and this system would maintain close ties with the state administration. The establishment of the villagers' self-governing system is thus a new strategy and important component of state administration.

The current villagers' self-governing system reflects some new characteristics and trends of rural politics and power structure in post-earthbound.

First, villagers' self-governing is actually a system implemented to meet the demands of modernization and democratization, and it has changed the general laissez-faire condition of rural administration. As a formality, it helps to satisfy the procedural needs of modern democratic governance; at the same time, it is a crucial component of the state institution, allowing the government to play a bigger role in grassroots society.

Second, the implementation of villagers' self-governing implies the establishment of a new social order. A set of standardized legal regulations replaces local customs, conventions and rituals as the basis of maintaining social order. While the latter may remain influential in the social, political, and economic life of some rural communities, their role as the foundation for grassroots social order is replaced by the modern state's political and legal systems.

Lastly, the establishment of villagers' self-governing has no doubt changed the mechanism of social control in traditional earthbound society. "Rule by elders" that is central to an earthbound society may remain somewhat influential in some areas and affairs, but they would no longer be the core authority in current rural society. While judicial authority is not yet the main force controlling order in rural society, the authority of grassroots administration does play a leading role in maintaining social control and realizing social justice. This is evinced by more villagers opting to turn to village cadres and the judicial system to resolve disputes and seek redress for injustice.[31]

The system and organizations of villagers' self-governing are greatly different from village autonomy in traditional earthbound society. As a legal institution of the modern state, villagers' self-governing is an extension of state administration. In traditional earthbound rural society, village autonomy relies on endogenous forces of the village for administration, even though state forces did have some reach over villages.

Moving forward into the new era, should the administration of rural communities follow village autonomy or and state governance? This is a dilemma that is also shared in the question of rural development. An overly simplified answer to this question may result in complex problems in the process of rural transformation and development, as well as a low estimate on their potential negative impacts. State governance had, in fact, been implemented in the people's commune and Great Leap Forward campaigns, and their results are clearly far from ideal. In the new era, however, simply choosing village autonomy is also not realistic either, nor is it definitely ideal. Perhaps, a flexible strategy of adopting to the local conditions and circumstances would help to find an ideal point of balance between the two approaches.

Agricultural development or industrialization

Another dilemma in rural development is whether to further develop agriculture to stimulate the growth of rural income and development, or to develop industrialization to allow peasants to grow affluent and transform the appearance of villages? If agricultural development is to be relied upon, what are the ways by which peasants can achieve continuously income growth? What kind of agricultural production would be capable of meeting the desires and needs for peasants to grow affluent? These are questions touching the core of rural development, because, on the macro perspective, the foundational position of agriculture in China's social development is untouchable, and so the sustained development of agriculture is the precondition for further general development. Under such conditions, the relationship between agricultural and rural development must be resolved; that is, to find a way to allow farmers to achieve steady income growth while maintaining steady agricultural development.

For a big country like China, ensuring national food security is essential, which means that the foundational position of agriculture must be maintained. Unfortunately, against the backdrop of marketization, agriculture is at a disadvantage because of its low relative profitability. Thus, reinforcing or even just sustaining the foundational position of agriculture faces many challenges. On the one hand, there is a necessity to encourage farmers to actively develop agricultural production; on the other hand, farmers need to be given opportunities to increase income and further their own development.

Currently, one difficulty facing agricultural development is the question of how to enable farmers to obtain a relatively ideal and steady income growth from agricultural production. Modern farming technologies, including crossbreeding, fertilizers, pesticides, and advanced horticultural techniques, have allowed agricultural yield to rise, despite shrinking arable land. The increase of agricultural production, however, has not been followed by income growth and increased efficiency for rural households; and marginal profitability for agriculture remains comparatively low. This affects, to some extent, farmers' confidence and enthusiasm. Therefore, in resolving the obstacles to agricultural development, the most important aspect is to raise the marginal profitability and relative economic efficiency of agricultural production. If agricultural income and economic efficiency were to remain much lower than commerce and industries, there would be a lack of incentives for farmers to actively maintain agricultural production, and there would be a lack of drive for further agricultural development.

Some regional governments try to help farmers increase income and efficiency by implementing two kinds of "top-down design" or development plan: one, invest in modern high-efficiency agriculture techniques, introducing new factors of production to raise income and economic efficiency; two, industrialize villages, helping to establish rural township enterprises to provide opportunities for farmers to increase their income.

Since the mid-1980s, township enterprises have sprung up in villages of southeastern coastal provinces, rapidly changing the economic structure of rural society and contributing to the rapid growth of the national economy. This industrialization path, however, was cut out from special circumstances. Fei pointed out that the rapid growth of rural township enterprises is the result of farmers "leaving the soil but not the village," as surplus labor looked for development opportunities while the urban-rural divide in household registration system limited their movement into cities, leaving farmers little choice but to develop industries in villages.[32] Indeed, industrialized rural areas have been so successful in achieving affluence and there is basically no agriculture in these villages. There are even some villagers who participate in neither agricultural nor non-agricultural production; instead, they have formed a new class of landlords who derive income from housing or land rentals, as well as collective bonus payouts and interests.

The particular success for these regions, however, does not mean that this should be taken as the trend in rural development. Overindustrialization of villages will lead to unthinkable consequences, as there would be a serious lack of domestic food supply, as well as huge losses of land which is suitable for producing safe food. Thus, rural industrialization can only be a localized strategy, and cannot be taken as an actual trend for rural development.

In fact, some regional and grassroots governments have actually tried to develop rural industries to help sustain rural income growth, but they failed to achieve expected targets, simply because not all villages are equipped with the conditions necessary to complement the development of industries.

Managing both the development of agriculture and industries is thus a problematic challenge for rural development. On the one hand, maintaining the current state of agricultural production and economic structure clearly does not contribute to rural development, let alone satisfying the need for rural income growth. On the other hand, taking the path of industrialization may result in various other problems: Whether industries can be developed in the first place; whether negative environmental impacts can be resolved; and whether rural industrial development can be sustained.

During the Cultural Revolution, the idea of conducting both agricultural and industrial production at the same time was floated, such that people's communes and production brigades were encouraged to conduct industrial construction on top of agricultural production. Soon there were actually collective enterprises run by people's communes and production brigades appearing in some villages, which gradually transitioned to township enterprises after the launch of the Reform and Opening Up policy. This strategy might in theory be an ideal solution for the agricultural-industrial quandary, but it is not generally applicable. The case that Ebenezer Howard's garden city philosophy fails to gain mainstream popularity shows how real world developments, even in Western countries, do not follow ideal scenarios. Howard expected to solve all the problems resulting from urbanization and industrialization with a third alternative, in which "all the advantages of the most energetic and active town life, with all the beauty and delight of the country, may be secured in perfect combination,"[33] and since garden cities were supposed to be more appealing than large cities, problems induced by the concentration of population in cities could be thereby avoided. But Howard's garden city turns out to be just a utopia, and Western industrialized society remains on the path of urbanization and industrialization, leading to overpopulation in cities while rural communities dies out.

There is thus no single principle to decide between agriculture and industrialization in the implementation of rural development. Instead, flexible measures suiting local conditions are needed, in order to allow rural communities to find the optimal equilibrium for agricultural development and rural income growth. This would, in theory, be the intersection where the curve of villagers' marginal income meets the curve of marginal agriculture costs. That is to say, if industrial development for a region shows diminishing marginal returns, while the price of agricultural loss paid for developing industries shows increasing costs, then the intersection of these two curves is the optimal point for maintaining both agriculture production and industrialization development. Since the marginal costs and returns for developing industrialization varies with different regions, it must once again be stressed that the development plans must suit local conditions.

Sustaining villages or allowing them to die out

In this era of urbanization and modernization, the future of China's rural development faces the most challenging question yet: Should villages be kept alive in the modern society or should they be allowed to die out in the process of urbanization? If villages are to be sustained, what should be done to stimulate its further development? On the other hand, if they are allowed to die out, how would the massive rural residents be settled, and can the structure of society maintain its integrity? Will there be great underlying risks in a society with no rural community?

Rural society does not necessary imply that its members are employed in agricultural production, but rather, a relatively closed and isolated society entity, independent relative to urban society. The uniqueness and peculiarity of rural society is exhibited in the countryside lifestyle, which contrasts starkly from the urban lifestyle, not just in terms of material differences, but also in cultural and social structures. Compared to urban areas, villages only have relatively poor public infrastructure, thus the conditions and standards of living are of a lower level. Much progress is being made as villages continue to modernize and urbanize, not only in terms of infrastructure, but also various other aspects such as culture and society. But this raises another worrying issue: Can rural society survive the changes brought about by modernization? What exactly is the future for village societies?

From the perspective of modernization theory, the modernization of traditional villages is an irreversible trend; and rural urbanization signals the end of village communities, which points to the direction of development and progress. For multicultural theory and nostalgia, however, the end of rural society is a case of modernity causing a huge loss to human culture. The survival of villages or village society is of great significance in preserving social and cultural diversity, while rural society as the basic unit of social life plays an active role in maintaining the balance of ecology and the environment.

The history of industrialized countries shows that there is no standard end point to rural development. Rural America becomes "non-farming rural zones," while rural France develops into "farms without farming." Just like what Mendras has said, French countryside "will be neither suburbs nor 'non-farming rural' zones as the Americans call them, but residential country"; there will be both persons who live without producing, or toil away all day long only to earn a meager income; the latter would never let land go wasted, or to put it in another way, allow the countryside to become "farms without farming."[34]

In Japanese and South Korea, industrialization, modernization and urbanization have turned villages into city suburbs. Even though their governments introduced an new community movement in the 1970s to revitalize rural communities, they could only revive villages as a form, but not as functional rural society.

In China, urbanization has progressed rapidly since the launch of Reform and Opening Up policy, especially with the establishment of the market economy. The dualistic urban-rural *hukou* system has, however, seen no changes in its legal status. During the 17th National Congress of the Communist Party of China, progressive implementation of urbanization, integrated with the rural reconstruction strategy, was proposed as the basic strategy guiding the development of the Three Rural Issues. By 2010, urbanization in China had reached 49.9%, in comparison with the 19.4% in 1980 — growing by an average of 1% annually.[35] Under the impact of rapid urbanization, what would be the end point of China's rural society? Would the urbanization process lead to population concentration towards cities, or suburbanization of villages? Is village society also facing a gradual demise? With the high rate of urbanization, there is no doubt that many villages have indeed disappeared. Past experience suggests that there are mainly three causes for the disappearing of village society: First, villages that were located on the peripheries of cities might have been assimilated into urban society; second, some remote villages may have slowing declined and disappeared with most of their population having migrated; and third, there are also some state-led mergers of villages to facilitate development.[36]

As the current level of urbanization in China is virtually half of the country, the state of China's rural society could to some extent be said to be at a crossroads, facing the question of whether to progress further in the direction of urbanization, or to sustain the existence of what remains of rural society. If the complete demise of China's villages is to be halted, what are the available ways to achieve this? As people increasingly pursue a modern and urban lifestyle, rural society will face a decline, and to reverse this trend and maintain the existence of rural society, the problem of rural development must be resolved. On the other hand, if urbanization and modernization were to be completely avoided, how would rural communities be able to receive a level of development comparable to cities? Thus, the conflict between sustaining rural society and urbanization is also a thorny development dilemma. Historically, most industrialized countries took the simplest solution: developing urbanization and the market mechanism. Given China's long agricultural tradition, however, this may not be a feasible solution. Furthermore, it might be wise to plan and selectively protect rural society, maintaining village societies with unique characteristics and culture. This would be a great contribution towards preserving human civilization, as opposed to the complete functional destruction of diverse rural cultures of American Indians by the U.S. As a developing country, China would do well to learn the lessons of developed countries and avoid the errors and trappings in the urbanization progress.

Summary and Discussions

"Earthbound China" is a concise generalization made by Fei about the nature and feature of China's rural society in the first half of the 20th century, or in other words, the social and cultural traits of the grassroots Chinese society in the pre-modernization period. Yet under the impacts of modernization, urbanization, marketization, and globalization, the earthbound society has already gone through structural transformation. Today, villages, as a relatively independent social community, preserve only parts of rural features, though their structural configuration remains the same. In this sense, China's rural society has transformed into a post-earthbound society.

Post-earthbound China is unique in two ways: First, from a dynamic sequential prospective, post-earthbound society is a manifestation of rural features in modern times, that is to say, China's rural society has moved from tradition to modernity; second, from a static structural point of view, post-earthbound villages are characterized by the structural transformation of rural social space, which is reflected in the co-existence of structural and institutional duality. Structural duality refers to the separation between urban and rural economic structures and between traditional and modern social structures. Institutional duality refers to the discriminatory arrangements between public and nonpublic sectors. With this characteristic of a double-dual pattern, rural life differs greatly from urban life, and rural migrants are excluded from the public sector and lead a highly uncertain life in cities.

The post-earthbound rural China is no longer recognized as being traditional, partially closed, and highly immobile; instead, it has become active in social transformation and high in mobility. This change has brought villages internal stratification and massive labor outflow. In post-earthbound rural society, the differential mode of association has changed as well, and the social network is no longer the combination of family members and relatives spreading out from a self. With extensive exchanges and frequent migrations, the circle of relationships has been extended beyond just kinship relationships, and fellow countrymen and power relations are now important components of people's social network.

In post-earthbound China, social order at the grassroots level is no longer maintained by rituals. Although rituals and conventions are still existing and influential in certain respects of rural society, they are no longer the foundation of social order. In the development of grassroots regime, the management of rural social order has become a part of the modern public management system of the country. The social order of the post-earthbound China is now under administrative and institutionalized control.

The system of self-governance in villages has further changed the power structure and political life of rural society. Direct elections of village leaders and the establishment of rural grassroots organizations have gained their legitimacy in the modern democratic system. The resulting village leaders and organizations have won the power to manage rural affairs through practice, thus completely overthrowing the dominance of paternalism.

Modernization and the double-dual pattern are what transform rural China into a post-earthbound society. Yet, post-earthbound China is merely a partially-transformed and partially-modernized rural society.

Post-earthbound China is faced with various dilemmas in its development, such as the choices between a rule of rituals and a rule of law, self-governing and state-governing, sustaining villages and terminating villages, as well as sticking to agricultural production and heading towards industrialization. To promote rural development, China must carefully weigh between both sides of the choices and prepare for the possible consequences. No one development model is universally applicable and the route to better rural development is many and various.

15

Chapter

Innovations in Market Institutions and Recent Rural Developments in China

The Three Rural Issues are inherently a problem of rural development. In what direction should peasants, villages, and the agricultural sector look to develop? Is there an ideal path that they could choose to take? These questions all involve some exploration of the path of the future development of rural communities. Rural development is an organic process that follows the regularities and mechanisms of social transformation, rather than a product of artificial design and construction. Finding the ideal path for rural development is essentially a study of the conditions underlying the natural development of rural communities, and also about coming up with better approaches of development based on these conditions. Such an exercise would, of course, not simply be a search for a unique optimal solution, but an act of finding a multitude of possible ways for building an ideal rural society. This chapter will provide a theoretical and empirical discussion on the institutions, policies, and measures that would help to address the Three Rural Issues, and explore the various paths towards the future of rural development.

China's Different Paths towards Rural Development

In discussing the problem of rural development, the question of the path or direction of development will inevitably crop up: it is not uncommon to think of having set goals and planned road maps as necessary in moving towards the future. The fact, though, is that the future of society is defined by current actions, while any goals and plans for the future are easily tainted by subjective ideals, such that the choice of the development path is often a point of contention among individuals with conflicting ideals.

In the early years of the PRC, it was common policymaking practice to link rural policies with the path of rural development. The debate over the path of rural development used to be highly politically charged, focusing on whether to take a more socialist or capitalist road; this is due to a fixed mentality that political choices determines everything, a legacy of China's decades of revolution-charged politics.[1] This conflict does reflect an ideological disagreement, but it may not necessarily be caused by political thought, which, in a way, is merely a vehicle for political conflict. For example, China's *1st Five-Year Plan* detailed specific arrangements for the rural system and policies, including the land system, food policy, and agricultural operation system, but changing rural policy would obviously upset established interests, and decision makers may also have different views with regards to the new institutional arrangements and policies. The challenge, then, was to legitimize and rationalize the new system and policies, and politicizing the issue of the path of rural development was both an expression and a strategy for achieving this. The period that immediately followed the revolution's victory was a time of political fervor among the populace, making it effective to politicize the approaches of rural development, even to a class struggle level. Once the new policies were labeled as "socialist" and any contrasting proposals would be denounced as "opposing socialism," the new system and policies became political symbols which were considered as sacredly inviolable, thus attaining legitimacy and popular support.

When rural reforms were first introduced, the issue of the path of development resurfaced, although this time the focus of the debate revolved mostly around whether to promote a collective economy or a household driven individual economy. Proponents of the collective economy believed that as a form of cooperative economy, the collective economy is more advanced compared to the small-scale individual economy, and that it is the general direction in which the future of rural development is headed. According to reformists who advocated the individual operation system, collective economy dampens farmers' motivation for production, leading to agricultural recession and even a shortage of food supply; individual economy where peasants operate independently, on the other hand, would be more effective in organizing agricultural productivity, eliminating the negative impacts of collectivism on farming enthusiasm, boosting agricultural production and economic performance, as well as pulling villagers out of destitution.

There is always a tendency to seek an ideal solution for the Three Rural Issues, yet it is utopian to believe that we could achieve the best result of rural development by sticking to the optimal principle or path. In reality, social development is a process in which different problems will present themselves at different stages of development, and each problem could be addressed in more ways than one. The optimal solution comes from integrating effective measures from multiple approaches; overidealized schemes, on the other hand, often end up as extreme approaches.

The debate between collectivism and individualism is theoretically antagonistic, but in reality, they coexist in a rural economy. For example, in post-reform Huaxi Village in Jiangsu Province, parts of the collective economy were retained and even further developed upon, fundamentally improving the appearance of the village;[2] at the same time, the village also implemented the household responsibility system, allowing individual operation in agricultural production. It can thus be seen that collective and individual economies can coexist and work well together, and they do not necessarily conflict with each other.

The reception to and results of the economic system varies with villages. After initially contracting out two collective enterprises to individuals, the village of Nanjie in Henan Province withdrew the contract rights in 1984 and returned to the development of the collectives, which resulted in a tax growth from CNY70,000 in 1984 to CNY60,000,000 in 1994, equivalent to 1,000 fold increase in production.[3] On the other hand, collectivism was highly unpopular in Xiaogang Village, Anhui province, making the development of a collective economy unworkable even with strong external backing from the government and other social forces. Here, it was the individual household economy that flourished, as the village sustained a significantly higher agricultural yield than during the collectivism period, shedding its past of destitution and its Three Relies label.[4] If collectivism were to be forcibly re-implemented in Xiaogang Village, it would no doubt be a huge blow to the autonomy and motivation of production for its villagers; one need not look deeply into the history for what the results would be in that case.

All these real life cases show that China's rural development is not about choosing a single structural mode of development or between collectivism and individualism. Elements of the two can coexist in a village, although some villages may show a preference for either one of the systems. Villagers' choices are determined by their social and economic conditions, rather than simple visions that are mere theoretical constructs. Thus, it is really an imposition of subjective construction to treat collectivism or individualism as the direction, path, or ideal of rural development, and the ideological debate on rural development is virtually irresolvable and practically worthless.

Collective economies work in some places because its mechanism of division of labor is able to raise efficiency in these places; if real economic division of labor and economies of scale cannot be achieved, then development of collective economies will increase costs and hurt the innovation and motivation of individual peasants. On the other hand, the success of individual economies is the result of its mechanism that protects individual autonomy and innovation and stimulates production motivation in the household responsibility system. Its lack of effectiveness in promoting division of labor means that it cannot be considered an ideal mode, much less to say the future path, of China's rural development.

The issue of rural development also attracts another debate between formalism and substantivism in the field of economic sociology and anthropology. In the context of rural development, formalism is closely related to Smithian and Marxist models:[5] Rural development follows the laws of market economy development, and the rural society can achieve an overall improvement by promoting commodity economy. Popkin's notion of the "rational peasant" asserts that traditional peasants are rational in making economic decisions and do not behave distinctively.[6] Similarly, Schultz noted that, in traditional agricultural production, the distribution of production factors was rarely inefficient.[7] Even though in many rural societies that were in chronic poverty, peasants grew the same crops with the same techniques on the same plots and appeared numb to market prices and economic stimuli, they often did a great job in efficiently distributing their production factors. Why, then, did these peasants rarely make use of new production factors and change their operation model, so that they could obtain higher income and escape poverty? Schultz argues that it is not a matter of knowledge or reluctance: The costs of new production factors are in reality prohibitive to the common peasant, meaning that poor peasants can only maintain their original operation model.[8]

Substantivism is concerned with the actual conditions, qualities, and beliefs surrounding humans and their conduct of economics. Within the discussion on rural development, substantivism stresses the social and cultural distinctions between agrarian and modern society, implying that rural development should stay on its own unique path rather than follow the principles and strategies of modernization. The most representative substantivists are probably Robert Redfield and James Scott. Redfield regards peasant society as a relatively closed "small community"[9] that has its own cultural traits — their "little traditions" — which by itself constitutes its own holistic social system. Although small communities exist within the large society, communicating with the large society in various ways, while also being impacted by developments in the large society, their development may still follow their own unique laws and characteristics. Following the behavioral logic of peasants, Scott further expounds on the social and productive distinctions between peasant society and modern society. Based on his research on peasant societies in Southeast Asian countries such as Vietnam, Scott proposes that the logic and principles behind peasant production is distinct from those followed by modern production organizations. According to Weber, the most significant feature of modern bureaucracy is the rationalization of organizational behavior.[10] In economics, this refers to the pursuit of maximized utility, while in sociology, it refers to the pursuit of rational goals and values. Scott finds that in the history of peasant society development, peasants do not prioritize the maximization of profits in organizing agricultural production. In some cases where production costs such as rent and loans are extremely high, operating production would not only result in virtually no profit margin but also run the risk of losses and bankruptcy; yet even under such circumstances, peasants still rent and borrow to maintain production. Why do they follow irrational principles of action? Or perhaps, why do the peasants' principles of action differ from rational principles? In Scott's theory, the reason is that for all rural households, keeping the family fed is their top priority, and it conforms to their principles of food security and subsistence ethics; in other words, before making a choice, peasants will first consider if this choice can help or hurt their livelihood. The peasant economy is thus a subsistence economy where ensuring the basic survival of the household is prioritized over economics.[11]

In a way, the formalist versus substantivist debate is also a kind of dualistic perception of the rural development issue. As pointed out by Levi-Strauss, binary opposition is the fundamental way for human to understand the world, and it is associated with the fundamental traits of human and their relation with nature.[12] People tend to understand things by putting them under two opposite categories: left or right, yes or no, black or white, and right or wrong. Formalism assumes the principle of rational choice as pure and ideal: Rational behavior is considered to be decisive in social and rural development, including market development, industrialization, urbanization, and organization, which in turn drive economic efficiency and boost rural development. In the real world, however, unified, ideal modes of social development do not exist; it is the exploratory actions of society members that actually contribute to the unique development of different regions and societies.

Substantivism stresses the particularities of peasant society. These particularities always exist, yet they are not incompatible with the common traits of development, such as markets and institutions which prove to be helpful in raising efficiency. Even though social actions of peasants are earthbound, their action choices do not actually deviate from the principle of rational choice: Peasants behave rationally in allocating their production factors and arranging social customs. Their principles of subsistence ethics and food security are, in fact, manifestations of rational choice under their actual circumstances.

Neither formalism nor substantivism should be considered as the exclusive and ideal path for China's rural development. An overaggressive pursuit of formalist ideals could lead to the neglect of actual social conditions and subsequent extreme behavior, while overemphasis on substantivism might result in missed development opportunities. Following either extremity will only impose artificial limitations on actual social development. If, however, China can avoid going into the aforementioned extremities, actively apply new technologies, and make adjustments according to local conditions, it will be able to carve its own way of rural development.

To break off from the dualist debates, some scholars have tried a "third way" or a "middle way" of rural development. For instance, Huang questioned whether China's villages, which developed under the incentives of increased autonomy and market stimulus in the 1980s into the basic unit of industrialized agriculture, can truly represent a new path of rural modernization that neither fits a socialist nor a capitalist path of development. Giddens also raised the possibility of a "third way" from the ideological dualism that dominates contemporary world politics,[13] noting that:

> The idea of finding a third way in politics has become a focus of controversy across the world.... During the Cold War period, many saw social democracy itself as a third way, distinct from American market liberalism on the one side and Soviet communism on the other.[14]

The "third way" was greatly advocated by the U.S. Democratic Party and the British Labour Party (especially during Blair's term) as a good combination of sustaining economic vibrancy and promoting social solidarity.

The idea of the "third way" or "middle way" is itself heavily political and ideological, because it is based on the assumption that rural or social development faces the problem of choosing between either a socialist or capitalist road. The logic is that neither socialism nor capitalism is ideal, and a middle way in-between, or a third way, may help to avoid the problems resulting from choosing one path over the other, and eventually lead to a sound development.

Classical Marxist social development theory views the distinction between capitalism and socialism not as different paths, but as different phases of historical development. Although Marxism also considers socialism and capitalism as representative of different social systems and mode of development, it does not treat them as particular systems in themselves: Market economy, industrialization, and urbanization can all be developed in socialist and capitalist societies.

Even though the "third way" or "middle way" appears in a way as a mediator in the ideological conflict over social development, its emergence has in fact strengthened the ideological meaning of social actions. Since the beginning of the Reform and Opening Up policy, coastal villages in Southeastern China have made impressive improvements economically and socially, and this presents a good case from which experience and methods could be drawn upon. But to view this phenomenon from the perspective of socialist-capitalist dualism, or even define its neutrality between the two, would in fact lead us back into the quagmire of ideological and subjective presumptions.

The development path of rural China should be confined to neither choosing from any given paths nor chasing a utopian model. Paths are cut out by walking through them; likewise, successful development can only be achieved through effective practical action. Predetermining an ideal, singular path would likely be nothing more than creating barriers and resistance to rural development. There are multiple ways and methods of bringing further rural development, and what is important is to identify the ones that are most effective.

The Choice between New Rural Communities and Urbanization

The issue of China's rural development has spawned two prominent and contrasting views: one advocating building new rural communities, and the other endorsing urbanization.

In 2006, the Central Committee of the CPC called for the construction of a new socialist countryside, whose ultimate goals were set as "developed production, well-off lives, cultured countryside, organized villages, and democratic administration,"[15] implying that the strategy of rural development will in the foreseeable future be focused on the reconstruction, construction, and development of villages, with the aim of affording villages a new look for life and future development.

The proposed new socialist countryside strategy is based on the idea of sustaining villages and promoting rural development. While China draws inspiration from the new community movement in Japan and South Korea in the 1970s, the significance of China's program is far greater for the country, because for a heavily populated country like China, the Three Rural Issues stand in an unshakable, fundamental position. No matter what route of development China takes, the development of the Three Rural Issues has to always keep up with the times, considering its positive role in maintaining a stable and harmonious society in China and developing a healthy global community. In this sense, it is rational to insist on promoting sustainable rural development.

Furthermore, it is unrealistic and extremely risky for China to marginalize or even abandon the rural economy even if against the background of globalization, industrialization and urbanization. Obviously, it is impossible to just abolish village communities for a foreseeable period of time, but more importantly, a rapid decay and disappearance of villages would lead to the loss of a vital, organic system of human sustenance, presenting an incalculable risk to a country as large as China. Sustaining and promoting the growth of villages, then, is hardly just for nostalgic reasons, for in fact, villages hold an enormous share of China's population, and they shoulder the crucial responsibility of supplying food and labor to a modernizing country. Thus, however challenging and difficult it is, China should sustain its villages, be devoted to the idea of constructing a new socialist countryside, and promote rural development.

The alternative view is that the direction and future of rural development lies in urbanization. In modernization theory, urbanization is regarded as the general trend of social development and a core indicator of the social modernization.

According to the theory of modernization, a society must undergo industrialization and urbanization to realize development. Modernization theory is a generalized hypothesis of social development patterns and future trends, which is based on the past and current events of social development with parts of it being facts while others reasonable assumptions. The modernization process does seem to be the main theme of contemporary social development, and the development of any society is in fact an effort to realize modernization. Urbanization is both the power engine and result of modernization, and it impacts not only social and economic structures, but also people's mind-set. As a crucial component of the social system, rural society is also subject to the influences of modernization and urbanization. It is thus necessary and significant for China to consider its rural development strategies and policies against the backdrop of modernization and globalization, in order to take advantage of the powers and mechanisms of urbanization and achieve more effective rural development.

Urbanization is a process where people shift towards working non-agricultural jobs, living in urban centers, and adopting a modern lifestyle. It is often accompanied by industrialization, and as industrial and commercial enterprises agglomerate in a certain region, the population will also gravitate towards the region, forming a populated urban center.

Urbanization is so much more than just population concentration in demographic and geographical senses. It signifies the transformation from an agricultural-rural civilization to an industrial-urban civilization, and represents the general trend and direction of social development. It is the both the process and result of social structural transition. From the perspective of urbanization, then, the development path of the future of villages does not only lie in developing villages themselves, but also in finding new ways to exist with the transformation and development of the urban-rural structure. Thus, institutional arrangements for promoting rural development require the consideration of the broader implications of urbanization and its role in developing villages.

Some of the main functional implications of urbanization in rural development are:

- Urbanization could drive a boom in the qualitative development of villages. The renewal of rural infrastructure or the new development of villages is not just about changing the appearance of villages, building new houses, paving new roads, or increasing household income by a few hundred yuan. Such quantitative changes are what Huang calls "rural involution" or "growth without development."[16] What rural society needs is a qualitative breakthrough in the development of its structure. Here, structural development refers to the new changes made in the entire social structure, including industrial structure, occupational structure, urban-rural structure, and cultural structure. Rural China should develop its predominantly agricultural economy to be more oriented towards the secondary and tertiary sectors, and change the traditional labor intensive model of agriculture to one that utilizes capital, technology, and information. As the level of urbanization rises, the new social structure will generate more non-rural employment, which will lead to a rise in the income levels of rural households. This would in turn change the lifestyle, culture, and beliefs in rural villages, creating more space and opportunities for further development.

- Urbanization is vital in providing effective production factors for rural development. Urban centers provide division of labor and a market mechanism that greatly raises the allocation efficiency of resources, such that the capital, technology, and information from urban regions and the labor, land, and natural resources from rural regions can be fully and optimally allocated.

  The pattern of rural development in Jiangsu and Zhejiang provinces shows that the rise of industry and commerce in villages drives the development of small towns, which is a form of urbanization. This mode may not be applicable to the whole nation, yet it does show that urbanization is a significant direction and driving force of rural development. Urbanization will lead to the reallocation of rural resources, during which process production efficiency rises and resources value appreciates. With rural resources growing more valuable, rural households have their sources of income multiplied and manage to earn more income, becoming economically prepared for further rural development.
- Urbanization can provide social subjects — villagers — with new platforms and opportunities for further development. The core of rural development lies in the development of rural residents, and all social development can be said to be ultimately a means to achieve maximal development and better welfare for the individuals in society. Thus, only when villagers see their economic, social, and cultural situations improved, can there be real rural progress.

  The key issue in the current state of rural development is the outward movement and development of rural labor. According to David Cale Johnson, an agricultural economist, China needs to transfer another two thirds of its agricultural labor force and maintains only about 100 million in agricultural production.[17] This number is rather unreachable under the present conditions: On the one hand, existing cities do not have the capacity to achieve a one-time absorption of such a huge amount of rural labor; on the other hand, this contingent of rural labor faces its own difficulties in migrating to cities directly. This means that urbanization must be relied on to gradually absorb surplus rural labor.

Urbanization is a dynamic process that involves the continuous expansion of existing cities, the transformation of rural communities into urban communities, as well as the interaction between urban and rural communities. It is not simply a matter of changing a rural populace into an urban one, nor of villagers moving into cities, but rather a structural modernization of traditional agriculture and rural society with increasing human capital in the rural populace. The urbanization strategy is thus a structural strategy, stimulating the co-development of rural and urban areas by adjusting the urban-rural and industrial structures.

- Urbanization would also push for changes in rural culture and life. Rural development not only involves developing its economy and society, but also its culture, beliefs, and lifestyle. A modernized and urbanized rural culture will help to drive further rural development. The evolution of rural lifestyle will change the structure of social behavior and impact the transformation and development of the rural social system.

Urbanization is a fundamental issue of rural development that needs to be addressed in order to truly grasp the direction of rural development and avoid missteps. The relationship between the rural and urban regions should not be viewed in a static vacuum, nor approached with a dualistic perspective on their development. Rural development and urbanization are co-moving and mutually interactive dynamic processes, and it is through the interaction and mutual integration between urban and rural regions that rural development shall be achieved.

Of course, while urbanization is vital to rural development, it must not be superficially seen as the absolute, exclusive path, nor should the narrow sense of urbanization be considered as the ultimate goal in rural development. It is a strong provider of the impetus for conducting development, but while it is an effective choice of development, it is certainly not the only path or the ultimate goal. More importantly, in the precise execution of urbanization as a way of rural development, it will be necessary to implement different policies and measures based on actual local conditions.

Considering the diversity of rural development paths, China not only has multiple ways of conducting urbanization, but also a number of alternatives to go about rural development. Strategic concepts on new rural construction and development is already being put into practice, but whether or not this would lead to the ideal development goal remains to be seen. In terms of diversity, however, it is clear that preserving and renewing the development of the rural community is not only strategically vital for China, but also for human society and culture as a whole. As the fundamental mode of human sustenance, rural communities hold a rich heritage of civilization and culture. Amidst the wave of modernization that has shocked and challenged the rural life, the need for cultural preservation and sustainable development means that new rural construction and development to integrate rural society with the modern life has become a necessary task.

Different Paths towards Urbanization

In China, the advancement of urbanization as a way of conducting rural development often raises worries from some policymakers, administrators, and urban residents. Would the influx of some seven to eight hundred million people from the countryside cause a population explosion in the cities? Would this not lead to the so-called "urban disease" as in Latin American countries?

These worries are, in fact, groundless, for they presume a static view that urbanization is just about transforming rural residents into urban dwellers or turning villages into towns or cities. If this were the case, urbanization would no doubt bring about numerous problems, yet this is not really what urbanization means.

First, urbanization is not just about population migration, but rather structural transformation in work, society, culture, and lifestyle. Promoting rural development through urbanization does not mean the transfer of rural residents into cities or the transformation of villages into towns or villages either in administrative title or form. The key to effective urbanization is to better coordinate the interaction between rural and urban communities and raise the overall level of urbanization in the entire society.

Second, the way to urbanization is not limited to a single choice. The movement of labor and population towards urban areas is only one way by which urbanization is manifested. As expansive as China is, the basic conditions and cultural background of each region can vary greatly, so individual regions should plot out its own development path towards urbanization based on its own conditions, whether it is the transformation of villages to cities or the building of new socialist countryside.

Historically, rural development and urbanization in other countries have also followed varied paths of development. For a big country like China, villages in each region are quite different in terms of natural conditions, historical and cultural traditions, as well as socio-economic situations. China's villages can learn from existing urbanization paths to carve out their own way of urbanization based local conditions. The reason why urbanization is said to be an effective approach to China's rural development is that urbanization can be achieved through diversified ways.[18]

Based on geographical and natural conditions, China's vast rural area can be divided into nine regions: Northeast, Northwest, North, East, Central, West, Southeast, South, and Southwest, each with its own unique characteristics and conditions.

- Northeast

  This region has a solid industrial foundation and plenty of fertile land. Here, urbanization should make full use of local industrial and agricultural advantages, developing modern farms and expanding industrial and agricultural markets. By doing so, villages in the northeast region can raise productivity and stimulate restructuring of industrial composition.
- North

  This region has a long history of agricultural production, and it is blessed with vast plains, convenient transportation, and dense population. The foundational position of rural development in North China is of enormous significance, especially in ensuring food security. To achieve urbanization, villages in this region should fully rely on their historical traditions and geographical advantages, while introducing modern factors of production such as advanced farming technology, production tools, and an agricultural market system. This development mode entails the urbanization of rural lifestyle.

  Rural North China features mostly plains with a high population density; people live in each other's neighborhood, and keep a tradition of village fairs. All these are favorable conditions for realizing the urbanization of rural lifestyle. With further improvement of rural public infrastructure, public administration system, social welfare and security systems, those villages will be able to thrive with a new outlook and social function.
- East

  Industrial development in the east has progressed relatively quickly, resulting in a high level of urbanization. The rural development of this region should make full use of the strong labor demand created by rapid industrial development to actively promote the urbanization of rural labor and rural society and avoid a separation between industrialization and urbanization. This region is in fact urbanization-ready, but the key obstacle is in institutional arrangements. It is thus necessary to eliminate urban-rural dualism and the *hukou* system and actively urbanize the rural labor force.

- Southeast

  The southeast coastal area is densely populated but short of land; industry and commerce have developed rapidly ever since the mid-1980s, especially with the rise of township enterprises, which have created plenty of opportunities for the transfer of rural labor to non-agricultural employments. Small towns have sprang up and opened up a unique path of development which features "leaving the soil without leaving villages."[19] This mode of urbanization is pioneered in southern Jiangsu and Wenzhou, where rural population does not migrate to cities, but undertakes non-agricultural activities, which helps the villages to expand its non-agricultural markets and develop minor townships.
- South

  Like the eastern region, Southern China possesses similar conditions and level of rural development. Villages of this regions can also rely on industrialization while deepening reform and opening up, improving institutional arrangements, eliminating institutional obstacles, and lowering the social costs of urbanization, so that villages can move quickly and smoothly on the track of urbanization.
- Central

  Agricultural production remains an integral part of the central region's economy. While it has a relatively high population density, it does not have the same farmable land per capita as the northern and northeastern regions; compounded with limited natural conditions of geography and climate, the productivity and economic efficiency of its villages is far from ideal. At the same time, even though this region is rich in surplus rural labor, its industrial and commercial development lags behind the eastern, southeastern, and southern regions. Rural development here may need to take a "middle way" — constructing new villages to promote the urbanization of village lifestyle, while promoting the development of central cities and urban-rural integration to allow rural and urban areas to develop in mutual symbiosis.
- Northwest and Southwest

  These two regions share some similarities in their environment and basic conditions. They are rich in natural resources, situated in border areas, resided by ethnically diverse populations, and dependent on featured agriculture and industry. They can, therefore, carve out their own way of urbanization by conducting border trade, developing a market of specialized products, and boosting local tourism.
- West

  Villages in Western China are mostly distributed in highlands and mountainous areas, where the conditions for agricultural productivity are poor, and the standard of living in villages low. This region does not have sufficient strength to drive rural development on its own, and needs help from external forces. For example, the national strategy of Western Development has proven successful in stimulating the development of rural areas in Western China, significantly upgrading the infrastructure and living facilities in the agricultural and pastoral areas. The region needs to take full advantage of the national development project, channeling more investment into rural human capital to allow its population to expand outwards and urbanize; at the same time, it should also rely on policy support and gradually realize the transfer of rural population and urbanization through land reforms and favorable migration policies. In highlands and mountainous areas, the government can integrate environmental protection and reforestation polices in order to push for the transfer of rural land and population resettlement and help the construction of small towns, realizing the rearrangement of resources, population and social structure.

In choosing the path of rural development, regional difference is a significant, yet not the only factor that needs to be considered. Other factors such as historical and present developments in economy and society may also be different greatly even among villages in similar regions. Villages, thus, should take into account of their local conditions when plotting out their own paths of urbanization, and then if this is coupled with institutional innovations, a multitude of ways to effectively promote rural development and urbanization will be produced. In summary, the current reality of rural development in China will mostly focus on three paths: urbanization of rural lifestyles, urbanization of villages into townships, and integration of urban and rural areas. These three paths will be vital to the effective development of present and future rural development in China.

Urbanization of rural lifestyle

The urbanization of rural lifestyle refers to the transformation of the rural way of life into a modern and urban one, without changing their living space and structure; that is, a spiritual rather than physical transformation. Urbanization is not all about relocating urban dwellers to urban areas, and modernizing the cultural beliefs and lifestyles of the rural population is, in fact, also a form of urbanization.

For a country with a huge rural population, it is an economical and efficient way to realize urbanization by simply urbanizing rural lifestyle. This approach can fundamentally remove the obstacles hindering the development of both rural residents and rural society, while preventing drastic geographical and spatial movement and restructuring of the general population. This alleviates the stress on development and social restructuring problems resulting from massive rural migration, which in turn greatly lowers the costs of development.

This approach is suitable for villages situated on plains that are well developed in agricultural production and are densely populated. While pursuing social development, these villages also need to sustain the foundational position of agriculture, both of which could be achieved through the urbanization of rural lifestyle. However, taking this approach requires the consideration of three aspects of development:

- Investment in public goods and construction of public facilities
  Low investment in public goods such as transportation and communication facilities not only constrains rural economic development and growth of rural income, but also directly impacts the quality of life in rural society. Public infrastructure in villages must be improved to provide the physical conditions necessary for raising the standard of living in villages.
- Education
  The low level of rural education is what impedes the urbanization of rural lifestyle. How much education people get is decisive in shaping their ideas and behaviors. A modern education in culture, knowledge, and technology is necessary for the modernization of beliefs and lifestyle.
  Rural education in China is currently underdeveloped, and to change this situation, the government needs to channel more investments in developing rural education, building a more comprehensive system of education in villages. Compulsory education should be extended to higher secondary education, including vocational training. It should also expand on adult education and vocational training in order to reduce and eventually eliminate adult illiteracy.
- Public administration
  In contrast to the public and social administration system that organizes urban society, rural society mainly relies on moral norms and social conventions developed based on social relations of familiarity to govern social order.

The above three respects are particularly important for promoting the urbanization of rural lifestyles, as they constitute the most significant differences between urban and rural developments. The major attraction for rural migrants to live in cities is the better living conditions that cities can offer. Thus, if villages can properly address the above issues and provide rural residents the life quality that matches up to that of cites, urbanization will be in fact realized.

Market town construction

The development of villages into market towns has become a common phenomenon in the development of rural society, representing both a trend and a mode of rural development. In the course of China's social transformation, the composition of the populace has changed dramatically due to the continued implementation of population control policies and the massive population migration driven by the Reform and Opening Up policy.

There is currently an estimated 200 million rural migrant workers moving between urban and rural areas, some of whom stay in cities on a long term basis. This has brought huge changes to the structure of rural population. Seniors, housewives, and children increasingly make up the majority of permanent residents in villages, while many young adults from remote rural areas are gradually concentrated in nearby towns and cities.

In recent years, villagers in some regions have greatly increased their income and savings through non-agricultural activities such as finding employment in the industrial, commercial, and service sectors away from home. This has enabled some rural households to purchase real estate and retail properties in towns, stimulating the growth of towns through the real estate market, contributing to the concentration of villagers towards towns. In addition to that, the springing-up of town enterprises adds ice on the cake, creating more employment opportunities for migrated villagers.

Given the major transformation of rural population composition and economic development, actively driving the development of villages into towns is of paramount significance. While this approach suits the actual needs of a majority of regions, certain issues regarding the different aspects of development still need to be addressed:

- The relationship between rural development and the construction of market towns

  The overall planning and execution of village reconstruction must be based on a perspective that benefits the long-term development of each village. If the construction of market towns is set as the goal of rural development by a certain region, then this region should put turning villages into market towns as its priority, utilizing the construction of market towns and rural market centers to drive the development of villages. In other words, village reconstruction has to revolve around the town center, stimulating the centralization of the village economy and social life.
- The relationship between infrastructure construction and institutional development

While the construction of infrastructure is necessary for the development of towns, it is also imperative to develop a corresponding institution that systematizes the reallocation, exploitation, and usage of the available land resources. Lack of work in this aspect would not only lead to the failure of new constructions to raise productivity, but even create new problems for future development. Therefore, the construction of market towns must be accompanied by systematical and rational institutional development to ensure a satisfactory result.

- The relationship between endogenous and exogenous development

  The construction and development of towns may be endogenous and spontaneous in regions that are more economically developed. With the increase of household income and savings, the motive of villagers to seek better development opportunities outside rural areas is reinforced, but for those whose accumulated capital is not enough for making investments in cities, they will choose to purchase real estate in nearby market towns, making a departure from the household economy. In such a way, more and more rural residents will be attracted to settle down in market towns, accelerating the development of towns. Since this kind of development is driven by the internal forces of rural society, it is considered to be endogenous.

  On the other hand, in places with an underdeveloped economy, exogenous development is more appropriate. That is because most of the population in those villages only makes a relatively low income and can barely sustain the basics of livelihood, thus unable to make any non-agricultural investment, let alone finance the transition of villages to market towns. Considering this, external assistance is needed to drive the construction of market towns, raise the supply and utility efficiency of public goods, and improve the life quality of villagers. Among the external forces, government financing should play a leading role. At the same time, the government can implement preferential policies to encourage other social forces to participate in the development of towns in these regions, such as tax relief on land use and industry and commerce. Additional policies for poverty alleviation and migration would also be needed to encourage the movement of impoverished villagers to resettle in towns.

- The relationship between industrial development and the construction of market towns

  The construction of market towns is in fact a step towards and an approach of realizing urbanization. The purpose of developing market towns is not just to concentrate villagers to towns, but more importantly, to help them transition into non-agricultural jobs. The construction of market towns must, therefore, be accompanied by corresponding industrial development and restructuring in order to provide sufficient non-agricultural employment opportunities for rural migrants. A large town area without sufficient non-agricultural industries would lead to surplus labor and low agricultural productivity, adversely impacting the progress of rural development and urbanization.

Developing villages into market towns is a way of urbanization widely suitable for many rural regions in China. Along the economically developed southeastern coast, towns are already established with rich historical traditions, and they have undergone further development in the process of rural industrialization. Integrating their development with the reconstruction of villages and improving their public infrastructure and administration institution would further elevate the level of urbanization of its villages.

For underdeveloped regions in Western China, it is also economical to promote urbanization by constructing market towns. By integrating rural reconstruction with the government's grand scheme of Western Development, these regions can make full use of poverty alleviation and environmental protection policies, as well as the strength of the government in a leading role in construction, to actively promote the development of market towns and encourage its population to concentrate towards towns. This would not only raise the living standards of villagers, but also fundamentally solve the problem of rural development in the western part of the country.

Urban-rural integration

Urban-rural integration could be said to be a fundamental path for rural urbanization and development: It encompasses both structural and institutional development necessary for eliminating the long standing dualism of China's society and institution, which has divided the country into two distinguishing systems of economy, society, culture, education, and administration. This dualism has greatly impeded the progress of urbanization as well as the development of villages and villagers. Since the implementation of the Reform and Opening Up policy, agricultural production has increased and the national economy has maintained its growth, but urban-rural disparity has been worsening. In 2007, the disposable income per capita of urban households is 3.33 times the net income per capita of rural households.[20]

The escalated lagging behind of rural development is actually a result of the long-term separation between urban-industrial development and urbanization; that is, industries and cities have developed, but peripheral rural areas and their inhabitants have not enjoyed a similar development. A great many rural residents have "entered" urban factories, obtaining non-agricultural jobs, yet they never really have "entered" cities, in the sense of becoming urbanized. This paradox of rural workers working in cities but not being considered urban citizens is exactly the result of the urban-rural dualistic institution, which gives rise to the imbalanced and uncoordinated structural development. The negative impacts of urban-rural dualism are mainly manifested in three aspects:

- Rural residents do not enjoy the same level of social welfare and security as urban residents, and the amount of public goods and welfare provided by public financing is far less in villages than in cities.
- Rural residents are rejected by the urban system. During the planned economy period, urban employment opportunities categorically exclude those holding a rural *hukou*, but even today, remnants of the old institution still effectively discriminate rural residents as a matter of habit. While rural residents are free to move to cities to live and operate businesses, their legal and social statuses are still outside the urban institution; that is, they are considered as foreigners or migrants.
- Public input from the government has been focused on urban infrastructure and development, while rural infrastructure and development has received relatively little investment.

The institutional flaws that have led to the prominent condition of the rural plight and the continued widening of the urban-rural gap have provoked much attention and debate. Urban-rural integration is thus a path of reforming and innovating the old institution, in order to create a favorable environment for urbanization and rural development. Some of the major aspects in this process are:

- The gradual elimination of the urban-rural institutional barrier should be implemented to promote the integration of rural migrant labor into urban society. While a large number of rural workers have shifted to urban non-agricultural occupations, institutional barriers have limited their further development and urbanization prospects, which in turn constrains the development of villages. Reforming the urban labor market system and social administration system will help more than 200 million rural migrant workers to gradually urbanize.
- Prefecture-level cities should play a central role in reforming urban financial and administrative systems to realize a unified budget for the provision of public goods within the jurisdiction of each prefecture-level city, balancing the supply of public goods between rural and urban areas. In particular, a good balance in public investment must be maintained in the fields of compulsory education, public health, infrastructure, social welfare facilities

such as nursing homes, and basic living security.

- The development of villages into towns should be integrated into the unified development plan of the central city, gradually building an urban nexus around the central city. This would allow for a centralized planning of the industrial layout, town distribution, and environmental development in relation to the city's strategic positioning, facilitating the orderly transfer of rural population towards towns. The development of the central city will drive the development of peripheral rural areas, organically linking the development of urban and rural areas and raising the urbanization level of villages.

The development of villages into towns may not be the only path towards rural development, but it can offer some effective solutions for the development of villages, and the way of constructing towns is not limited to just one. China has vast rural areas with huge regional differences, and this fact makes it impossible for villages in China to develop into a unified mode of towns in a short period of time. From a development perspective, however, villages should be given the opportunity to develop into a modern and urban society regardless of regional differences in conditions. The development of towns should thus be planned and conducted based on particular conditions and advantages of individual regions, instead of pursuing a unified model of development

When exploring their own path of development, villages can utilize the approaches and measures inspired by the development of towns according to local natural and social conditions. At the same time, traditional forces and methods are insufficient, and so relying on the momentum from the development of towns could be an effective path in promoting rural development.

Innovations in Market Institutions and Recent Rural Developments in China

Reviewing the history of rural development since the implementation of the Reform and Opening Up policy, the achievements in rural development can be found to be intricately linked to the developments of the market. Its role in stimulating rural development is mainly exhibited in the opening up of three major markets: the market for rural agricultural products, the market for rural industrial products, and the urban labor market.

The opening of the rural agricultural market means that farmers can now expand their production beyond fulfilling national quotas and sustaining household livelihoods. During the collective economy period, farmers were not allowed to produce for the market: Such behavior was not only branded as "capitalist," but also severely regulated through institutional arrangements. While the institutional change brought about by rural reforms are apparently manifested in the transition from collective operations to household contracting, on a macro perspective, the rapid development of the rural economy and society has been achieved mostly through the market. For example, the first areas and households to grow in wealth after the implementation of rural reforms achieved their success mainly through the rapid development of specialized agricultural production. In rural areas where operations of scale, specialized planting, and animal farming were developed, most rural households were able to become specialized producers, escaping poverty and becoming wealthy in a short period of time.

The successful development of rural areas and households through the opening of agricultural product markets is not exactly widespread, and relatively speaking, villages situated in the southeast coastal region, near big cities, and easily accessible to public transport are more likely to benefit from that. But, it is still theoretically possible for all villages of different conditions to have their local agricultural production flourished, if they can find a way to access the big market or even the global market.

With the opening of the rural industrial product market, some villages and households have made a qualitative leap in rural development by taking the road of industrialization; in other words, these villages developed industrial production while maintaining agricultural production. One of the model cases is the southern Jiangsu Province. Villages in this region are densely populated and have a rather solid base of agricultural production. Since the mid-1980s, township enterprises and private enterprises run by rural households have sprung up in this region, which have helped quantitatively improve the situations of the small-peasant economy and the life of small-peasant households. This contrasts starkly with the phenomenon of "rural involution" or "growth without development" found by Huang,[21] as the problem is solved through rural industrialization, allowing for rapid development of village society and villagers, raising the standard of living and modernizing the culture and lifestyle in village society. Therefore, villages of southern Jiangsu Province make a miracle thanks to the open and progressing market of non-agricultural products. And this piece of experience also shows that China shall seek its rural development in all sorts of markets, not simply the market of agricultural products.

The case of South Suzhou as a model of rural development reflects the role of non-agricultural product markets in driving the rural development. It proves that both collective and individual operations can drive the development of villages and villagers, as long as the mode of operation can successfully establish itself and develop in the non-agricultural product market. In rural areas that are densely populated and suboptimal for agriculture, rural involution will occur if the community does not expand beyond the agricultural market; the success of South Suzhou villages is fundamentally attributable to the opening and development of the non-agricultural product market. Thus, one key aspect to rural development is for rural residents to be able to obtain more opportunities outside the agricultural product market.

The success of the household responsibility system reform in driving the development of the Three Rural Issues lies in its liberation of rural labor and opening up of the urban labor market. Free from the constraints of collective production and labor, villagers can choose, based on the principle of rational choice, a more productive and profitable mode of production, which leads to a rise in rural economic efficiency. The opening of the urban labor market provides opportunities for rural labor to obtain higher efficiency: When the profit opportunity in villages is limited, rural workers can take up opportunities provided by the urban labor market to increase personal income.

Presently, many rural regions are indeed utilizing the urban labor market for new development opportunities: The opening of the urban labor market has allowed for the influx of large numbers of rural migrant workers into cities, who are thus able to increase their household income. But while some have successfully integrated into urban society and achieved further development, the majority of rural workers remain circular migrants, and their limited opportunities of development are fraught with uncertainty.

The history of rural development illustrates how the opening and development of markets is a vital driver of new rural development. However, the development of rural markets has not always been smooth, and market opportunities fluctuate with uncertainty at different periods of time. Some markets could be highly open at certain stages, while being heavily regulated at other stages. Market development does not necessarily follow its own logic and regularities; instead, it may be under the influence and constraints of various factors, particularly institutional or policy factors. Institutions can define the boundary of current choices for independent economic agents, define the relationship between individual subjects, and specify the limitations of actions. Since they define the set of choices available to groups and individuals, they occupy the central position at all choices and behavior. The collection of institutional arrangements determine economic conditions at specific times; that is, all economies would have a central collection of standards, rules, regulations, conventions, and legal structure that defines the set of choices available to groups and individuals.[22]

It can thus be seen that a relevant institutional foundation is necessary for rural markets to achieve stable and sustainable development, where the institutional boundaries can define a relatively stable set of choices, keeping people's choice of actions predictable, so that decision making and collective actions will be neither random nor uncertain. In the real world, it is not uncommon to see "people governing policy"; that is, government policies and decisions change with leadership or administration. A market can be highly open today, and totally closed tomorrow with a simple shift in power. In this sense, the relation between market and institution is not as what North has suggested: Market failure is the primary reason for institutional changes. When the market fails to effectively regulate people's choice of actions through prices and supply and demand, new demand for institutional changes arises.[23] New institutionalism stresses innovation and endogeneity, arguing that "the appearance of various factor and commodity markets is one of the most significant institutional innovations in economic history.... The rise of factor markets is believed to be an institutional innovation resulting from the differences between different production units."[24] The basic assumption is that the economic system is highly independent, meaning that the evolution of the economic system almost fully follows its own logic and regularities. Historically and in the present, however, such a system can rarely be found, since changing from an old institution to a new one solely based on market demand and changes is extremely difficult to accomplish.

During the transformation of modern society, economic activities and systems are no longer embedded in social systems, but become quite independent.[25] However, economic activities and systems can never be completely independent from social systems. Economic activities are still more or less affected and constrained by political, social, and cultural factors, and economic systems are particularly vulnerable to political and ideological influences. The most efficient system is not necessarily a natural choice for a society; moreover, the efficiency of a system only becomes tangible in its operation. Thus, efficient institutional innovations would not emerge if without a pertinent institutional environment.

In a rural economic system — at least in present Chinese rural society — it is difficult for new factor and product markets to emerge naturally. Without relevant institutional force to drive changes, the progress of development of rural markets would be very slow, since the rural economic system has not developed to a state of relative independence. The relationship between the state and rural society remains intricate and peculiar, meaning that the role of politics on rural economy, and political factors on rural development should not be underestimated. Under such conditions, it is clearly unrealistic to expect institutional innovations of market development to emerge endogenously within the rural economic system. Thus, the state remains the main driving force behind institutional innovation in China's rural market; only when the state devotes resources to rural reconstruction and renewal of development, particularly marketization in rural areas, can significant and effective institutional innovation and changes occur.

Past successes in China's rural reforms have shown that the opening of the agricultural product market, the rural industrial product market, and the labor market, has been vital in providing development preconditions and market opportunities for the Three Rural Issues. Thus, to encourage more institutional innovations, China should continue to deepen reforms in this direction and go further down the path of opening and developing these three factor markets. This would involve reforms in the rural economic institution, as well as in the rural social administration institution, eliminating institutional mechanisms that constrain the emergence and development of new rural factor markets, in order to create a favorable institutional environment for the development of rural markets.

The development of rural markets is not only influenced by institutional mechanisms, but also other deep-lying structural factors. These structural constraints are more complex and challenging to solve, since the structure of rural society and culture cannot be fundamentally changed within a short period of time. Thus, institutional innovations should also pay attention to guiding and stimulating social and cultural transformation in villages.

As traditional factor markets in rural areas continue to open up and develop, the focus of rural market institutional innovations should be given to the development of new factor markets, such as the land circulation market, agricultural technology market, agricultural product market, and even the capital market. The emergence and development of these new markets will bring more development opportunities for the Three Rural Issues.

Institutional innovations aiming at building a market society should be conducted at three levels — the state, local governments, and grassroots administrations. The state should work in unifying the market system, legal system, and other macro policies; local governments should work with their local resources and endowed factors to build unique regional factor markets; grassroots administrations should support and encourage individuals of rural society to realize their innovations. If the three levels of efforts can coordinate with each other on an open and inclusive basis, a new era in the development of the rural market will arrive.

Discussions and Summary

Where should China's future rural development head towards? How can the country manage to get there successfully? These are questions need to be answered in order to pursue the further development of villages, and they are also at the core of the Three Rural Issues.

There are many ideological and theoretical disputes and contentions over the direction and path of China's future rural development: between socialism and capitalism, collective economy and individual operation, and formalism and substantivism. Even the proposal to develop a "third way,"[26] in fact, shares the same belief that there will be one and only one path for China's rural development. But while singular approaches seem to be more convenient to implement, they could turn out to be greatly incompatible with the realities in particular regions, ending up impeding rural development. It remains easy for theorists to remain trapped in the fantasy of finding a unified, systematic solution to the entire problem of China's rural development; Zhou, for example, accepts that "diversified reforms clearly reduce risks and raise the chances of success, while the imbalanced political, economic, and social development across China's vast expanse is also an objective basis for diversified reforms," but he still holds that "endorsement for diversification cannot exceed reasonable limits," and that in-depth rural reforms require a shared, standardized system and organization.[27] But it is precisely that singular paths thought to be bright and ideal that do not apply generally to different real world scenarios, often resulting in constrained development and high risk of failure. The discussion on rural development should thus escape the trappings of dualistic debates between exclusive perspectives, while the exploration for diversity in development direction and path should both remain rooted in the concerns of villages and jump outside of villages to expand the view of development to the context of the entire social system.

While urbanization has become the mainstream in rural development, this does not imply that other modes of rural development would definitely lead to failure. Whether rural development in China has to follow the path of ending villages and developing them into towns is, in fact, a momentous question worthy of more reflection and discussion, and it also directly impacts the way in which rural reconstruction and development shall be conducted. If China decides to sustain the existence of villages, then rural reconstruction should do more than just a simple facelift but inject new factors to vitalize rural development. On the other hand, rural reconstruction should not be treated as the only way to achieve rural development. Urbanization should also be recognized as a powerful driving force behind modern social development; it is through urbanization that the structure of society has transitioned from the traditional into the modern form. It is thus also a vital path in modernizing traditional agriculture and rural society. For China, historical conditions have limited its modernization project to heavily favor industrialization over urbanization; that is, it has had to stress economic modernization over social modernization. This has resulted in rapid economic development contrasted by frustrated social development, manifested in the phenomenon of rapidly increasing urban affluence while the development of rural communities lags behind, causing the continued widening of the urban-rural gap. Thus, the significance of urbanization not only lies in the development of rural regions through the development of towns, but also in the promotion of social integration.

Urbanization is also not limited to the simple urbanization of rural population. In particular, for a country as populous as China, achieving urbanization would be extremely challenging if it were to simply urbanize its rural population. However, the goal of urbanization could still be achieved, if villages choose diversified paths of development according to local conditions. Different modes of urbanization mainly include urbanizing rural lifestyles, developing villages into towns, and integrating urban and rural communities. Villages of different regions can rely on rural reconstruction to promote the urbanization of lifestyle and the development of towns, and at the same time, implement institutional innovations to help rural migrants integrated into urban society and facilitate the process of urban-rural integration. Increasing the level of urbanization will help to gradually alleviate the problems of the Three Rural Issues and the friction between urban and rural development.

Both rural reconstruction and urbanization require the driving force of the market mechanism. Marketization reforms in rural regions lead to the opening up of factor markets, which has stimulated rural economy and raised rural household income. The successful cases in China's rural reforms has shown that it is precisely the opening up of the rural agricultural product market, the rural industrial product market, and the urban labor market, that have greatly encouraged the growth of the rural economy since the launch of the Reform and Opening Up policy. To promote new rural development in the imminent future, more in-depth marketization reforms are needed to stimulate the continued development of rural markets, particularly the property market, technology market, commodities market, and the capital market.

The development of rural marketization is essentially a two-way opening up between rural communities and markets. This has fully taken advantage of the role of the market mechanism in efficient resource allocation to enable rural production factors and resources to attain a higher efficiency. The development of rural markets implies not only the construction and development of particular markets, but more importantly, the fostering and refining of the market system in rural communities. The operation and efficiency of markets are closely linked to relevant institutional arrangements, and therefore, institutional innovation is crucial for transforming the relatively underdeveloped rural markets.

Looking at past cases of rural market development, markets would develop extremely slowly if depending solely on endogenous factor price changes to drive institutional change. On the other hand, if the government were to enforce institutional changes to artificially accelerate market construction and development, there would be a high risk of planning or decision errors damaging the interests of rural communities. Perhaps, then, it would be more feasible for the government to compile the experiences and actual conditions of various regions and invest appropriately in market development, in order to induce and stimulate further development of rural markets.

The sluggish nature of China's rural market development and its present state are complexly interlinked. The key to escaping this entanglement lies in market institution innovation. It is only under the drive of institutional innovation and change that present modes of behavior and relationship structures that constitute economic and social development can be changed. In China where villages share a special connection with the government, the main driving force behind institutional innovation in rural markets mainly comes from the state. At the same time, innovation of the market institution should also be conducted at the regional and grassroots levels. When institutional innovations at all three levels coordinate with and reinforce each other, they would form a unified force empowering the rapid development of the rural market and rural society.

Notes

Chapter 12

1. Fei, *Peasant Life in China.*
2. Potter, *China's Legal System,* 14–15.
3. Crook and Crook, *Mass Movement in a Chinese Village: Ten Mile Inn.*
4. Du, *Land Reform in China.*
5. Luo, *The History of Land Reform in China.*
6. MacFarquhar and Fairbank, *The People's Republic, Part I: The Emergence of Revolutionary China, 1949–1965,* 87.
7. Du, *The Self-Account of Du Runsheng: Major Strategies in China's Rural Reforms,* 32.
8. Zhou, *Rural Reform and China's Development.*
9. Mao, "Two Talks on Mutual Aid and Co-operation in Agriculture."
10. Ibid.
11. Luo, *The History of Agricultural Collectivization.*
12. Lu, *Peasant China — Study of Post-Earthbound Society and New Rural Construction.*
13. Du, *The Self-Account of Du Runsheng: Major Strategies in China's Rural Reforms.*
14. Bo, *A Review of Major Decisions and Events.*
15. MacFarquhar and Fairbank, *The People's Republic, Part I: The Emergence of Revolutionary China, 1949–1965,* 304.
16. Wang, "The People's Commune Movement and the Transformation of Social Base of the Chinese Countryside."
17. Foreign Language Press, ed., *People's Communes in China,* 7.
18. Zhang, *Farewell to the Ideal: A Study on the People's Commune System,* 74.
19. National Bureau of Statistics of the People's Republic of China, *China Rural Statistical Yearbook 2008.*
20. Ibid.
21. Ibid.
22. Lu, *Embedded Politics and Economic Transition: The Case in Xiaogang Village, Anhui Province.*
23. National Bureau of Statistics of the People's Republic of China, *A Leap Forward: 30 Years of Rural Reform.*
24. Ibid.
25. National Bureau of Statistics of the People's Republic of China, *The Fourth Report of the Report Series for the 60th Anniversary of New China.*
26. Gan, *China Statistical Yearbook on Township Enterprises 2004.*
27. Fei, *Enriching the People — A Study of the Entire Country,* 544.
28. National Bureau of Statistics of the People's Republic of China, *China Rural Statistical Yearbook 2008.*
29. Wen, *Rural Construction Should Still Be Our Priority.*

Notes

Chapter 13

1. Lukács, *History and Class Consciousness: Studies in Marxist Dialectics*, 46.
2. Wright, *Classes.*
3. Lu, "Capital Logic and Social Structure of Contemporary China."
4. Fei, *Peasant Life in China.*
5. Huang, *The Peasant Economy and Social Change in North China.*
6. Zhao, *Changes in Li Village*, 51.
7. Crook and Crook, *Mass Movement in a Chinese Village: Ten Mile Inn.*
8. Lu, *Embedded Politics and Economic Transition: The Case of Xiaogang Village, Anhui Province.*
9. Okun, *Equality and Efficiency: The Big Tradeoff.*
10. Lu, *Embedded Politics and Economic Transition: The Case of Xiaogang Village, Anhui Province.*
11. Zheng and Wong, "The Issue of Rural-Urban Migrants in China: Theoretical Judgement and Policy Frame."
12. Li, *Urban Migrant Workers and Social Stratification in China.*
13. Lu, *Peasant China — Study of Post-Earthbound Society and New Rural Construction.*
14. Lu, *Research Report on Social Stratification in Modern China.*
15. Zheng, *Empirical Studies on the Social Stratification of Rural China.*
16. Nee, "The Emergency of a Market Society: Changing Mechanism of Stratification in China."

Chapter 14

1. Fei, *Peasant Life in China.*
2. Fei, *From the Soil: The Foundations of Chinese Society*, 37.
3. Lu, *Peasant China — Study of Post-Earthbound Society and New Rural Construction.*
4. Fei, *From the Soil: The Foundations of Chinese Society*, 37.
5. Ibid.
6. Ibid, 40.
7. Ibid, 39.
8. Ibid, 40.
9. Ibid, 40–41.
10. Feuchtwang, "What Is a Village?"
11. Zhao, *Closed and Open Circular Development: A Theoretical Framework for Understanding Earthbound China and its Transition.*
12. He, "The Semi-Acquaintance Society."
13. Bian, "Relational Sociology and Its Disciplinary Status."
14. Lu, *Peasant China — Study of Post-Earthbound Society and New Rural Construction.*
15. Lu, "A Village in Migrating: Double Duality and Indefiniteness of Rural Society — Social Condition of T Village in East Anhui Province."
16. Xiang, *The Community across the Border: Life in Beijing's "Zhejiang Village."*
17. Wang, *Social Mobility and Social Reconstruction: Beijing's "Zhejiang Village."*
18. Fei, *From the Soil: The Foundations of Chinese Society*, 60.
19. Ibid, 70.
20. Ibid, 69.

21. Ibid, 65.
22. Wang, *Culture and Power from the Perspective of Villages: A Case Study of Three Villages in Fujian and Taiwan.*
23. Lu, "A Village in Migrating: Double Duality and Indefiniteness of Rural Society — Social Condition of T Village in East Anhui Province."
24. Giddens, *The Third Way: The Renewal of Social Democracy.*
25. Fei, *From the Soil: The Foundations of Chinese Society*, 95.
26. Ibid, 94–100.
27. Huang, *Civil Justice in China: Representation and Practice in the Qing Dynasty.*
28. Ibid.
29. Fei, *From the Soil: The Foundations of Chinese Society*, 100.
30. Zhu and Nan, "Village Committees and Structural Changes of China's Rural Society."
31. Lu, "A study of Dispute Resolution in the Perspective of Legal Sociology: Problems and Paradigms."

Chapter 15

1. Huang, *The Peasant Family and Rural Development in the Yangzi Delta, 1350–1988.*
2. Zhou, *Huaxi Village: Post-Collectivism in a Transitional Economy.*
3. Xiang, *Village Administration under Collective Economy.*
4. Lu, *Embedded Politics and Economic Transition: The Case in Xiaogang Village, Anhui Province.*
   The Three Relies refers to the state that villages rely on state-resold grain for food, loans for production, and social relief for development.—Ed.
5. Huang, *The Peasant Family and Rural Development in the Yangzi Delta, 1350–1988.*
6. Popkin, *The Rational Peasant: The Political Economy of Rural Society in Vietnam*, 1.
7. Schultz, *Transforming Traditional Agriculture*, 33.
8. Ibid, 72.
9. Redfield, *The Little Community and Peasant Society and Culture*, 7.
10. Weber, *Economy and Society: An Outline of Interpretive Sociology.*
11. Scott, *The Moral Economy of the Peasant: Rebellion and Subsistence in Southeast Asia.*
12. Lévi-Strauss, *Structural Anthropology.*
13. Huang, *Involution and Modernization: Crisis of Normative Epistemology and Ways-out.*
14. Giddens, *The Third Way and its Critics*, 1.
15. Lu, "The Background, Pattern and Dilemma of Constructing New Socialist Countryside: A Sociological Understanding."
16. Huang, *The Peasant Family and Rural Development in the Yangzi Delta, 1350–1988.*
17. Johnson, "Elmhirst Memorial Lecture: The Limited but Essential Role of Government in Agriculture and Rural Life."
18. Lu, *Peasant China — Study of Post-Earthbound Society and New Rural Construction.*
19. Fei, *Selected Works of Fei Xiaotong.*
20. National Bureau of Statistics of the People's Republic of China, *China Rural Statistical Yearbook 2008.*
21. Huang, *The Peasant Family and Rural Development in the Yangzi Delta, 1350–1988.*

Notes

22. Bromley, *Economic Interests and Economic Institution: The Theoretical Foundation of Public Policy.*
23. North, *Structure and Change in Economic History.*
24. Lin, *Institution, Technology, and China's Agricultural Development.*
25. Polanyi, *The Great Transformation: The Political and Economic Origins of Our Time.*
26. Huang, *Involution and Modernization: Crisis of Normative Epistemology and Ways-out.*
27. Zhou, *Property Right and Institutional Changes: Empirical Research on China's reform*, 68.

Bibliography

Chinese materials:

Bian Yanjie 邊燕傑. "Guanxi shehuixue ji qi xueke diwei" 關係社會學及其學科地位 [Relational Sociology and Its Disciplinary Status]. *Journal of Xi'an Jiaotong University (Social Sciences)* 西安交通大學學報 (社會科學版), (3) (2010).

Bo Yibo 薄一波. *Ruogan zhongda juece yu shijian de huigu (xia)* 若干重大決策與事件的回顧 (下) [A Review of Major Decisions and Events]. Vol.2. Beijing: People's Publishing House, 1993.

Du Runsheng 杜潤生. *Du Runsheng zishu: Zhongguo nongcun tizhi biange zhongda juece jishi* 杜潤生自述：中國農村體制變革重大決策紀實 [The Self-Account of Du Runsheng: Major Strategies in China's Rural Reforms]. Beijing: People's Publishing House, 2005.

———. *Zhongguo de tudi gaige* 中國的土地改革 [Land Reform in China]. Beijing: Contemporary China Publishing House, 1996.

Fei Xiaotong 費孝通. *Congshi qiuzhi lu* 從實求知錄 [Selected Works of Fei Xiaotong]. Beijing: Peking University Press, 1998.

———. *Zhizai fumin — Cong yanhai dao bianqu de kaocha* 志在富民——從沿海到邊區的考察 [Enriching the People — A Study of the Entire Country]. Shanghai: Shanghai People's Publishing House, 2007.

Gan Shiming 甘世明. *Zhongguo xiangzhen qiye nianjian 2004* 中國鄉鎮企業年鑒2004 [China Statistical Yearbook on Township Enterprises 2004]. Beijing: China Agriculture Press, 2004.

He Xuefeng 賀雪峰. "Lun ban shuren shehui" 論半熟人社會 [The Semi-Acquaintance Society]. *Cass Journal of Political Science* 政治學研究, (3) (2000).

Li Qiang 李強. *Nongmingong yu Zhongguo shehui fenceng* 農民工與中國社會分層 [Urban Migrant Workers and Social Stratification in China]. Beijing: Social Sciences Academic Press, 2004.

Lin Yifu 林毅夫. *Zai lun zhidu, jishu yu Zhongguo nongye de fazhan* 再論制度、技術與中國農業的發展 [Institution, Technology, and China's Agricultural Development]. Beijing: Peking University Press, 2000.

Lu Pinyue 魯品越. "Ziben luoji yu dangdai Zhongguo shehui jiegou quxiang" 資本邏輯與當代中國社會結構趨向 [Capital Logic and Social Structure of Contemporary China]. *Philosophical Researches* 哲學研究, (12) (2006).

Lu Xueyi 陸學藝. *Dangdai Zhongguo shehui jieceng yanjiu baogao* 當代中國社會階層研究報告 [Research Report on Social Stratification in Modern China]. Beijing: Social Sciences Academic Press, 2002.

Lu Yilong 陸益龍. "Jiufen jiejue de fa shehuixue yanjiu: Wenti he fanshi" 糾紛解決的法社會學研究：問題及範式 [A study of Dispute Resolution from the Perspective of Legal Sociology: Problems and Paradigms]. *Social Sciences in Hunan* 湖南社會科學, (1) (2009).

———. "Liudong de cunzhuang: Xiangtu shehui de shuang eryuan geju yu bu queding xing — Wan dong *T* cun de shehui xingtai" 流動的村莊：鄉土社會的雙二元格局與不確定性——皖東T村的社會形態. [A Village in Migrating: Double Duality and Indefiniteness of Rural Society — Social Condition of T Village in East Anhui Province]. *Journal of China Agricultural University (Social Sciences Edition)* 中國農業大學學報（社會科學版）, (1) (2008).

———. "Shehui zhuyi xin nongcun jianshe de beijing, moshi ji wuqu: Yizhong shehuixue de lijie" 社會主義新農村建設的背景、模式及誤區——一種社會學的理解 [The Background, Pattern and Dilemma of Constructing New Socialist Countryside: A Sociological Understanding]. *Journal of Peking University (Philosophy & Social Sciences)* 北京大學學報 (哲學社會科學版), (2) (2007).

———. *Nongmin Zhongguo: Hou xiangtu shehui yu xin nongcun jianshe yanjiu* 農民中國：後鄉土社會與新農村建設研究 [Peasant China — Study of Post-Earthbound Society and New Rural Construction]. Beijing: China Renmin University Press, 2010.

———. *Qianru xing zhengzhi yu cunluo jingji de bianqian – Anhui Xiaogang cun diaocha* 嵌入性政治與村落經濟的變遷——安徽小崗村調查 [Embedded Politics and Economic Transition: The Case of Xiaogang Village, Anhui Province]. Shanghai: Shanghai People's Publishing House, 2007.

Luo Pinghan 羅平漢. *Tudi gaige yundong shi* 土地改革運動史 [The History of Land Reform in China]. Fuzhou: Fujian People's Publishing House, 2005.

———. *Nongye hezuo hua yundong shi* 農業合作化運動史 [The History of Agricultural Collectivization]. Fuzhou: Fujian People's Publishing House, 2004.

National Bureau of Statistics of the People's Republic of China 中華人民共和國國家統計局. *Lishi de kuayue: Nongcun gaige kaifang 30 nian* 歷史的跨越：農村改革開放30年 [A Leap Forward: 30 Years of Rural Reform]. Beijing: China Statistics Press, 2008.

———. *Zhongguo nongcun tongji nianjian 2008* 中國農村統計年鑒2008 [China Rural Statistical Yearbook 2008]. Beijing: China Statistics Press, 2008.

———. *Zhongguo tongji nianjian* 中國統計年鑒 [China Statistical Yearbook]. Beijing: China Statistics Press, 2008 and 2011.

———. "Xin zhongguo chengli 60 zhounian xilie baogao zhi si: Chengxiang jumin shenghuo cong pinkun xiang xiaokang maijin" 新中國60周年系列報告之四：城鄉居民生活從貧困向全面小康邁進 [The Fourth Report of the Report Series for the 60th Anniversary of New China: From Poverty to Overall Well-off]. Accessed August 11, 2015. http://www.stats.gov.cn/ztjc/ztfx/qzxzgcl60zn/200909/t20090910_68636.html.

Tian Yipeng 田毅鵬. "'Cunluo zhongjie' yu nongmin de zai zuzhi hua" 「村落終結」與農民的再組織化 ["Disappearing Villages" and Farmer's Reorganization]. *The Journal of Humanities* 人文雜誌, (1) (2012).

Wang Chunguang 王春光. *Shehui liudong he shehui chonggou: Jingcheng 'Zhejiang cun' yanjiu.* 社會流動和社會重構 —— 京城"浙江村"研究 [Social Mobility and Social Reconstruction: Beijing's "Zhejiang Village"]. Hangzhou: Zhejiang People's Publishing House, 1995.

Wang Lisheng 王立勝. "Renmin gongshe hua yundong yu Zhongguo nongcun shehui jichu zaizao" 人民公社化運動與中國農村社會基礎再造 [The People's Commune Movement and the Transformation of Social Base of the Chinese Countryside]. *CPC History Studies* 中共黨史研究, (3) (2007).

Wang Mingming 王銘銘. *Cunluo shiye zhong de wenhua yu quanli: Min Tai san cun wu lun* 村落視野中的文化與權力——閩台三村五論 [Culture and Power from the Perspective of Villages: A Case Study of Three Villages in Fujian and Taiwan]. Beijing: SDX Joint Publishing Company, 1997.

Wen Tiejun. 溫鐵軍. "Women hai xuyao xiangcun jianshe" 我們還需要鄉村建設 [Rural Construction Should Still Be Our Priority]. *Open Times* 開放時代, (06) (2005).

Xiang Biao 項飙. *Kuayue bianjie de shequ: Beijing 'Zhejiang cun' de shenghuo shi* 跨越邊界的社區——北京"浙江村"的生活史 [The Community across the Border: Life in Beijing's "Zhejiang Village"]. Beijing: SDX Joint Publishing Company, 2000.

Xiang Jiquan 項繼權. *Jiti jingji beijing xia de xiangcun zhili* 集體經濟背景下的鄉村治理 [Village Administration under Collective Economy]. Wuhan: Huazhong Normal University Press, 2002.

Zhang Letian 張樂天. *Gaobie lixiang – Renmin gongshe zhidu yanjiu* 告別理想 —— 人民公社制度研究 [Farewell to the Ideal: A Study on the People's Commune System]. Shanghai: Oriental Publishing Center, 1998.

Zhao Shuli 趙樹理. "Lijiazhuang de bianqian" 李家莊的變遷 [Changes in Li Village]. In *Zhaoshuli xuanji* 趙樹理選集 [The Collection of Zhao Shuli]. Beijing: Beijing Yanshan Publishing House, 2006.

Zhao Xudong 趙旭東. "Bihe xing yu kaifang xing de huiquan fazhan: Yizhong lijie xiangtu Zhongguo ji qi zhuanbian de lilun jieshi kuangjia" 閉合性與開放性的迴圈發展：一種理解鄉土中國及其轉變的理論解釋框架 [Closed and Open Circular Development: A Theoretical Framework for Understanding

Earthbound China and its Transition]. *Open Times* 開放時代, (12) (2011).

Zheng Gongcheng 鄭功成 and Linda Wong 黃黎若蓮. "Zhongguo nongmingong wenti: Lilun panduan yu zhengce silu" 中國農民工問題：理論判斷與政策思路 [The Issue of Rural-Urban Migrants in China: Theoretical Judgement and Policy Frame]. *Journal of Renmin University of China* 中國人民大學學報, (6) (2006).

Zheng Hangzheng, 鄭杭正. *Dangdai Zhongguo nongcun shehui zhuanxing de shizheng yanjiu* 當代中國農村社會轉型的實證研究 [Empirical Studies on the Social Stratification of Rural China]. Beijing: China Renmin University Press, 1996.

Zhou Qiren 周其仁. *Chanquan yu zhidu bianqian: Zhongguo gaige de jingyan yanjiu* 產權與制度變遷——中國改革的經驗研究 [Property Right and Institutional Changes: Empirical Research on China's reform]. Beijing: Social Sciences Academic Press, 2002.

———. *Nongcun gaige yu Zhongguo fazhan* 農村改革與中國發展 [Rural Reform and China's Development]. Oxford: Oxford University Press, 1994.

Zhou Yi 周怡. *Zhongguo diyi cun: Huaxi cun jingji zhuanxing zhong de hou jiti zhuyi* 中國第一村：華西村經濟轉型中的後集體主義 [Huaxi Village: Post-Collectivism in a Transitional Economy]. Oxford: Oxford University Press, 2006.

Zhu Youhong 朱又紅 and Nan Yuzi 南裕子. "Cunmin weiyuanhui yu Zhongguo nongcun shehui jiegou bianqian" 村民委員會與中國農村社會結構變遷 [Village Committees and Structural Changes of China's Rural Society]. In *Xiandai hua jincheng zhong de Zhongguo nongmin* 現代化進程中的中國農民 [Farmers in the Process of China's Modernization]. Nanjing: Nanjing University Press, 1998.

English materials:

Crook, Isabel, and David Crook. *Mass Movement in a Chinese Village: Ten Mile Inn*. London: Routledge & Kegan Paul, 1979.

Fei Hsiao-tung [Fei Xiaotong]. *Peasant Life in China*. London: Kegan Paul, Trench, Trubner, 1939.

Feuchtwang, Stephan. "What Is a Village?" In *Cooperative and Collective* in *China's Rural Development: Between State and Private Interests*. Edited by Eduard B. Vermeer, Frank N. Pieke, and Woei lien Chong, 54. Armonk: M.E. Sharpe Inc., 1998.

Foreign Language Press, ed. *People's Communes in China*. Beijing: Foreign Language Press, 1958.

Giddens, Anthony. *The Third Way and Its Critics*. Cambridge: Polity Press, 1998.

———. *The Third Way: The Renewal of Social Democracy*. Cambridge: Polity Press, 1998.

Howard, Ebenezer. *Garden Cities of Tomorrow*. London: S. Sonnenschein & Co., 1902.

Huang, Philip C. C. *Civil Justice in China: Representation and Practice in the Qing Dynasty*. Redwood City: Stanford University Press, 1996.

———. *Involution and Modernization: Crisis of Normative Epistemology and Ways-out*. Shanghai: Shanghai Academy of Social Sciences Press, 1992.

———. *The Peasant Economy and Social Change in North China*. Stanford: Stanford University Press, 1985.

———. *The Peasant Family and Rural Development in the Yangzi Delta, 1350–1988*. Stanford, Calif.: Stanford University Press, 1990.

Johnson, David Gale. "Elmhirst Memorial Lecture: The Limited but Essential Role of Government in Agriculture and Rural Life." In *Agricultural Competitiveness: Market Forces and Policy Choice* (Proceedings of the Twenty-second International Conference of Agricultural Economists, Held at Harare, Zimbabwe, August 22–29, 1994). Edited by George H. Peters and Douglas D. Hedley, 8–21. Aldershot, Hants and Brookfield, Vt.: Dartmouth, 1995.

Lévi-Strauss, Claude. *Structural Anthropology*. New York: Basic Books, Inc., 1963.

MacFarquhar, Roderick, and John K. Fairbank, eds. *The People's Republic, Part I: The Emergence of Revolutionary China, 1949–1965*. Vol.14 of *The Cambridge History of China*. New York: Cambridge University Press, 1987.

Mao Tse-tung. "Two Talks on Mutual Aid and Co-Operation in Agriculture." In Vol. 5 of *Selected Works of Mao Tse-tung*. Accessed March 27, 2015. https://www.marxists.org/reference/archive/mao/selected-works/volume-5/mswv5_36.htm#v5_37

Nee, Victor. "The Emergency of a Market Society: Changing Mechanism of Stratification in China." *American Journal of Sociology*, (101) (1996).

North, Douglass. *Structure and Change in Economic History*. New York: Norton, 1981.

Okun, Arthu. *Equality and Efficiency: The Big Tradeoff*. Washington, D.C.: Brookings Institution Press, 1975.

Polanyi, Karl. *The Great Transformation: The Political and Economic Origins of Our Time*. Boston: Beacon Press, 1944.

Popkin, Samuel. *The Rational Peasant: The Political Economy of Rural Society in Vietnam*. Oakland: University of California Press, 1979.

Potter, Potman. *China's Legal System*, Cambridge: Polity Press, 2013.

Redfield, Robert. *The Little Community and Peasant Society and Culture*. Chicago: The University of Chicago Press, 1973.

Schultz, Theodore. *Transforming Traditional Agriculture*. New Haven: Yale University

Press, 1964.

Scott, James C. *The Moral Economy of the Peasant: Rebellion and Subsistence in Southeast Asia*. New Haven: Yale University Press, 1976.

Weber, Max. *Economy and Society: An Outline of Interpretive Sociology*. Oakland: University of California Press, 1978.

Wright, Erik Olin. *Classes*. London: Verso Books, 1985.

Translated materials:

Bromley, Daniel W. *Jingji liyi yu jingji zhidu: Gonggong zhengce de lilun jichu* 經濟利益與經濟制度：公共政策的理論基礎 [Economic Interests and Economic Institution: The Theoretical Foundation of Public Policy]. Translated by Chen Yu 陳鬱, et al. Shanghai: Shanghai People's Publishing House, 1994.

Fei Hsiao-tung [Fei Xiaotong]. *From the Soil: The Foundations of Chinese Society*. Translated from *Xiangtu Zhongguo* 鄉土中國, by Gary Hamilton and Wang Zheng. Berkeley: University of California Press, 1992.

Lukács, Georg. *History and Class Consciousness: Studies in Marxist Dialectics*. Translated from *Geschichte und Klassenbewußtsein: Studien über marxistische Dialektik*, by Rodney Livingstone. London: The Merlin Press, 1971.

Mendras, Henri. *Nongmin de zhongjie* 農民的終結 [The End of Peasants]. Translated from *La Fin Des Paysans*, by Li Peilin 李培林. Beijing: China Social Sciences Press, 2010.

Index

Index

CPSIA information can be obtained
at www.ICGtesting.com
Printed in the USA
LVOW03*0953030116
468496LV00017BA/250/P

9 781623 200862